A Creative Tension

Lee H. Hamilton served as a U.S. congressman from Indiana from 1965 to 1999, contributing significantly to foreign policy with particular interests in the former Soviet Union, Europe, and the Middle East. He was a member of the House Committee on International Relations for his entire tenure and served as ranking Democrat for ten years and chairman for two. Hamilton continues to influence U.S. policy and serves on the president's Homeland Security Advisory Council. Since 1999, he has been director of the Woodrow Wilson International Center for Scholars and director of the Center on Congress at Indiana University.

Jordan Tama, formerly special assistant to the director at the Woodrow Wilson Center, is a graduate student at the Woodrow Wilson School of Public and International Affairs at Princeton University.

WILSON FORUM

The Wilson Forum illuminates issues in public affairs with inquiry and experience. The essays in this series of brief books reflect on current questions through their history, their interplay with economics, politics, culture, and international relations, and their likely future course.

The Wilson Forum comes from the Woodrow Wilson International Center for Scholars, an institution in Washington, D.C., whose mission is to symbolize and strengthen the interaction between the world of scholarship and the world of public affairs. The Wilson Forum series draws on authors from both worlds, hoping to serve a broad audience of readers who share a desire to understand their world and take responsibility for its future.

Previously published
Democracy and the Internet: Allies or Adversaries?
by Leslie David Simon, Javier Corrales,
and Donald R. Wolfensberger

European Defense Cooperation: Asset or Threat to NATO?
by Michael Quinlan

A Creative Tension

The Foreign Policy Roles of the President and Congress

Lee H. Hamilton

with
Jordan Tama

Published by
Woodrow Wilson Center Press
Washington, D.C.

Distributed by
The Johns Hopkins University Press
Baltimore and London

Editorial Offices
Woodrow Wilson Center Press
One Woodrow Wilson Plaza
1300 Pennsylvania Avenue, N.W.
Washington, D.C. 20004-3027
Telephone: 202-691-4010
www.wilsoncenter.org

Order from
The Johns Hopkins University Press
P.O. Box 50370
Baltimore, Maryland 21211
Telephone: 1-800-537-5487
www.press.jhu.edu

This book draws from "The Making of U.S. Foreign Policy: The Roles of the President and Congress over Four Decades," by Lee H. Hamilton, in *Rivals for Power: Presidential–Congressional Relations*, 2d edition, edited by James A. Thurber (Lanham, Md.: Rowman and Littlefield, 2002). Used by permission of the publisher.

2 4 6 8 9 7 5 3 1

Cover Design by Naylor Design Inc.
Cover Photo by David Hawxhurst

Library of Congress Cataloging-in-Publication Data

Hamilton, Lee.
    A creative tension : the foreign policy roles of the President and Congress / Lee H. Hamilton with Jordan Tama.
    p. cm. — (Wilson forum)
Includes index.
    ISBN 1-930365-12-8 (alk. paper)
1. Presidents—United States.   2. United States. Congress.
3. United States—Foreign relations.   I. Tama, Jordan, 1976–
II. Title.   III. Series.
    JK585 .H365 2002
    327.73—dc21   2002012700

Contents

⚡ Acknowledgments

This book is the product of more than three decades of work on foreign policy, which I have conducted with the help of a great number of talented and dedicated people. My excellent congressional staff—too numerous to name here—provided me with the critical assistance, information, and recommendations that made my work in international affairs possible. Other members of Congress, officials in the executive branch, and experts outside government have also had a tremendous influence on my foreign policy views and actions over the years. My observations in the book reflect the contributions these many people have made to the development of my perspective on the foreign policy roles of the president and Congress.

Jordan Tama provided me with invaluable assistance in putting the book together, and Michael Van Dusen, Kenneth Nelson, Robert Hathaway, Martin Sletzinger, Chris Kojm, Don Wolfensberger, Louis Fisher, and James Thurber offered helpful comments on drafts. The observations made in the book are mine, however, and I take full responsibility for its content.

CHAPTER 1

✏ Introduction: New International Challenges and Opportunities

Some people have asked me over the years how an Indiana man like myself got involved in foreign policy. Today it might not seem unusual, because Americans of all backgrounds are involved in international affairs. But when I first entered Congress in 1965, foreign policy tended to be directed by an elite circle of experts and officials who came primarily from the Northeast.

I had no intention of becoming involved in foreign affairs. It happened purely by accident. I wanted to join a House committee involved in domestic issues, but was placed instead on the Foreign Affairs Committee. My experience there showed me that I enjoyed working on foreign policy, and I remained on the committee for my entire tenure in Congress—thirty-four years. At one point, I even turned down a spot on the powerful Ways and Means Committee, which nearly everybody in the House wants to be on, so that I could continue to work on international affairs.

Looking back now at my years of service in Congress, I am grateful that I was given the opportunity to contribute in some small measure to American foreign policy. I had the privilege to work with seven presidents, from Lyndon Johnson to Bill Clinton, and eleven secretaries of state. I was able to work on policy development through my chairmanships of several committees, including the Foreign Affairs Committee (now the International Relations Committee), the Permanent Select Committee on Intelligence, the Joint Economic Committee, and the Joint Committee on the Organization of Congress.

I tried to use my position in the House to help shape a sound American foreign policy that promotes peace, stability, democracy, market reform, and economic development. I am pleased that I was able to play a modest role in influencing U.S. foreign policy on issues such as U.S–Soviet relations, Arab–Israeli peace negotiations, arms control, and international trade. I also sought to improve the performance of Congress in foreign policy—for instance, by trying to reform the way it appropriates and oversees foreign aid.

One of the striking things about my congressional service is how much has changed since I first joined the House—in the congressional workload, the legislative process, and public policy issues. In the realm of foreign affairs, the Cold War and the conflict in Vietnam were America's dominant concerns in the mid-1960s. Every foreign policy issue was seen through the lens of the U.S. struggle against the Soviet Union and worldwide communism. Americans really did not know whether the Cold War would end peacefully, as it ultimately did, or in a horrific nuclear holocaust. Foreign policy making was largely the domain of a few powerful executive officials and congressional leaders, while the average member of Congress or ordinary American had little say in policy development.

Nearly four decades later, both the international environment and the foreign-policy-making process are dramatically different, though the basic goals of U.S. foreign policy and the central roles of Congress and the president remain the same.

The threat once posed by the Soviet Union is now gone, and America has new opportunities to advance its goals. Today's international environment is, for the most part, overwhelmingly beneficial to the United States, whose preeminence is not challenged seriously by any other nation. The great powers—Europe, Japan, China, Russia, and the United States—are generally seeking friendly relations with each other. Nearly all countries are moving toward free markets and democracy, if they have not adopted them already. International trade is expanding, respect for human rights is spreading, and the authority of international law is growing.

We face many dangers, however. The diversity of the security and economic threats around the globe is daunting. Terrorism, which has already struck the United States brutally, will be a continuing threat in the years ahead, and it may become more deadly if weapons of mass destruction proliferate and reach the wrong hands. The greatest security threat might be the danger that nuclear weapons or materials in Russia could be stolen and sold to terrorists or hostile nations and used against Americans at home or abroad. Groups and individuals that do not wish us well will also attempt to attack us with weapons of mass disruption, such as information warfare, which could assault our economic, financial, communications, information, transportation, or energy infrastructures.

There are numerous other threats to national security. The world's population will increase substantially during the first half of the twenty-first century, placing added strain on natural resources, including water, and possibly intensifying interstate conflicts and civil strife. Economic crises will likely be a regular occurrence, throwing some nations into turmoil and occasionally creating widespread financial instability. International crime, the illegal drug trade, global warming, infectious diseases, and other transnational problems will challenge national sovereignty and threaten our security, prosperity, and health.

Yet these dangerous threats are balanced by many opportunities. As the world's most powerful nation, the United States has a tremendous capacity to influence the world for good—to protect international peace, root out terrorism, resolve conflicts, spread prosperity, and advance democracy and freedom. Other nations look to us for leadership and to set an example of responsible and principled international action. Our values of freedom, justice, the rule of law, and equality of opportunity are increasingly the values of peoples around the globe. In the coming decades, the spread of these values and incredible advances in science and technology will give us the capacity to disseminate knowledge, cure diseases, reduce poverty, protect the environment, and create jobs in the farthest-flung corners of the world. So our new world is as full of hope as it is of danger.

To meet the threats and take advantage of the opportunities, the United States will need strong leadership, expertise in many fields, and large measures of foresight and resolve. Again and again, I have been impressed with the need for U.S. leadership on the most pressing international challenges. If something important has to be done—from fighting international terrorism to bringing peace to the Middle East—no other country can take our place. We may not get it right every time, but our leadership is usually constructive and helpful.

We must, however, be aware of the limits to American power. The United States is neither powerful enough to cause all of the world's ills, nor powerful enough to cure them. So it is critical that we maintain good relations with our international allies and friends, manage prudently our sometimes difficult relationships with Russia and China, and support and strengthen international institutions. A world that is committed to working together through effective international institutions and partnerships will be the world most capable of protecting peace and security and advancing prosperity and freedom.

Equally important for a successful foreign policy will be cooperation between the president and Congress. Today's moment of U.S. preeminence has not come to this nation by chance. Sound policies shaped by past presidents and Congresses helped to place us in this desirable position. To remain secure, prosperous, and free, the United States must continue to lead. That leadership requires the president and Congress to live up to their constitutional responsibilities to work together to craft a strong foreign policy.

The great constitutional scholar Edward Corwin noted that the Constitution is an invitation for the president and Congress to struggle for the privilege of directing foreign policy. Although the president is the principal foreign policy actor, the Constitution delegates more specific foreign policy powers to Congress than to the executive. It designates the president as commander-in-chief and head of the executive branch, whereas it gives Congress the power to declare war and the power of the purse. The president can negotiate treaties and nominate foreign policy officials, but the Senate must approve them. Congress is also granted the power to raise and support armies, establish rules on naturalization, regulate foreign commerce, and define and punish offenses on the high seas.

This shared constitutional responsibility presupposes that the president and Congress will work together to develop foreign policy, and it leaves the door open to both of them to assert their authority. On some basic foreign policy issues, the president and Congress agree on their respective roles. For instance, Congress generally does not question the president's power to manage diplomatic relations with other nations, and presidents accept that Congress must appropriate funds for diplomacy and defense. But on a panoply of other issues—from oversight of foreign aid and responsibility for trade policy to authorization of military deployments and funding for international institutions—Congress and the president battle intensely to exert influence and advance their priorities.

Of course, I approach the executive–legislative relationship from the perspective I gained during my congressional experience. That experience has convinced me that Congress plays a very important role in foreign policy, but does not always live up to its constitutional responsibilities. Its tendency too often has been either to defer to the president or to engage in foreign policy haphazardly. I recognize that political pressures, institutional dynamics, and the heavy domestic demands placed on Congress can make it difficult for it to exercise its foreign policy responsibilities effectively. But I believe that Congress could improve its foreign policy performance markedly if it made a concerted effort to do so.

Although the president is the chief foreign policy maker, Congress has a responsibility to be both an informed critic and a constructive partner of the president. The ideal established by the founders is neither for one branch to dominate the other nor for there to be an identity of views between them. Rather, the founders wisely sought to encourage a creative tension between the president and Congress that would produce policies that advance national interests and reflect the views of the American people. Sustained consultation between the president and Congress is the most important mechanism for fostering an effective foreign policy with broad support at home and respect and punch overseas. In a world of both danger and opportunity, we need such a foreign policy to advance our interests and values around the globe.

CHAPTER 2

Changes in the Making of Foreign Policy

The relative power of the president and Congress in foreign policy has fluctuated throughout U.S. history. At times, the president has assumed extensive power that has been largely unchecked by Congress. In other periods, Congress has asserted its constitutional authority and restricted the president's capacity to act on his own. Since the 1960s, the general trend has been toward greater congressional assertiveness, which has been fueled by changes in the international environment, American domestic politics, and the internal operations of Congress and the executive branch.

Historical Evolution

Throughout American history, the president has tended to wield the greatest power in foreign policy during times of national crisis, war, or heightened public interest in foreign affairs. The twentieth-century presidents who enjoyed the most control over foreign policy—Woodrow Wilson until 1919; Franklin Roosevelt after 1941; and Harry Truman, Dwight Eisenhower, John Kennedy, and Lyndon Johnson—governed during major wars or at the height of the Cold War. Similarly, George W. Bush assumed more foreign policy power after the attacks on the World Trade Center and Pentagon. Congress has tended to assert greater authority when the United States has been at peace and the American people have been more disengaged from world events, such as in the aftermath of World War I and during the decade following the end of the Cold War.

The founders delegated major foreign policy powers to both the president and Congress following the failed experiment under the Articles of Confederation, which had given responsibility for foreign policy to the legislature. During the nation's early decades under the Constitution, presidents such as George Washington and Thomas Jefferson exerted great influence over foreign policy—on issues ranging from relations with European powers to the Louisiana Purchase—though they came regularly to Congress to seek statutory authority for their actions. Except for the Civil War years, Congress gained the upper hand in foreign policy for most of the remainder of the nineteenth century, as the nation was consumed with domestic developments and expansion westward. The Senate's refusal to ratify an 1869 treaty regarding U.S. relations with Santo Domingo exemplified the strained congressional–executive relationship in foreign policy that characterized much of the second half of the 1800s.

In the early twentieth century, Presidents Theodore Roosevelt and Woodrow Wilson asserted greater presidential authority as they expanded the U.S. role in the world and brought the nation into World War I. Wilson's bold proposals for a new global collective security system marked a high point in presidential influence on the world stage, but they were followed by a new era of congressional ascendancy at home that began with the Senate's rejection of U.S. membership in the League of Nations in 1919. Congress held the upper hand during the interwar years of scaled-back U.S. involvement in international affairs, marked in the 1930s by the passage of neutrality acts and restrictive trade and immigration legislation.

The U.S. entry into World War II fostered a renewed presidential dominance of foreign policy, which lasted through the 1960s. During the war, President Franklin Roosevelt signed numerous executive orders, which do not require congressional approval, on issues such as arms sales to the United Kingdom and the future of Europe. President Harry Truman claimed a few years later that he did not need congressional authorization to send U.S. forces to Korea. Once, when asked who makes U.S. foreign policy, Truman replied simply, "I do." No American president would make that statement today, though many subsequent presidents have failed to appreciate fully Congress's foreign policy role.

Congress began to step up its involvement in foreign policy in the late 1960s and early 1970s. Its newfound assertiveness was fueled by frustration with executive branch secrecy and abuses by the administrations of Lyndon Johnson and Richard Nixon in Vietnam and elsewhere. Most members of Congress, and many of the American people, became concerned during the Vietnam War that the United States had moved too far and too fast in concentrating war-making and other powers in the hands of the president. Believing that such a concentration of power was not necessary, desirable, or tolerable in a democratic society, these members gradually sought to restrict presidential power and enhance the foreign policy influence of Congress.

I came to Congress as a supporter of the Vietnam War, but I developed concerns about its conduct after taking a congressional trip to Vietnam in the mid-1960s. I subsequently introduced one of the first amendments proposing to reduce the U.S. military commitment in that country. Televised hearings on Vietnam, first held by the Senate Foreign Relations Committee in 1966, raised more doubts about the war and further increased public opposition to it.

But Congress was slow to take dramatic action on Vietnam, in part because it was difficult for Congress to block funding for the war effort without holding up all appropriations for defense or denying U.S. combat forces the means to defend themselves. At the time, no amendments were allowed on defense appropriation bills, which were decided by a single yes–no vote. Many of us who had reservations about the war did not want to use the blunt, and politically unpopular, tool of rejecting entire defense appropriation bills.

By 1973, however, Congress changed its rules for considering defense appropriations and, with greater assertiveness, passed legislation that helped to end the war and establish a new framework for executive and legislative war-making authority. The War Powers Act of that year, passed over President Richard Nixon's veto by

284–135 in the House and 75–18 in the Senate, imposed groundbreaking procedural restraints on the capacity of the president to commit U.S. armed forces abroad. The act, which I supported, stipulates that the president must consult with Congress before introducing U.S. forces into hostilities or imminent hostilities, must report to Congress when such forces are introduced, and must terminate the use of forces within sixty to ninety days unless Congress authorizes their use or extends this period.

The War Powers Act's guiding principle is that the nation should go to war only with the consent of both the president and Congress. Those of us who supported it argued that it would help provide Congress with the means to fulfill the war-making responsibility assigned to the legislature by the Constitution. We also believed that it would provide Congress with a means to influence policy other than simply by withholding funds. The act has failed to live up to its promise, however, because presidents have not accepted its constitutionality and the president and Congress have often ignored its provisions.

Following the celebrated enactment of the War Powers Act, Congress continued to flex its foreign policy muscle. The Watergate scandal of 1973–74 weakened the personal position of President Nixon and the institutional power of the presidency, whereas revelations of secret Central Intelligence Agency (CIA) operations, such as support for the 1973 military coup in Chile, further emboldened Congress to take the offensive in ways it would not have considered a decade before. In 1974, Congress challenged administration policy on two major issues. First, following Turkey's invasion of Cyprus, it prohibited military aid to Turkey that was supported by Nixon and his successor, President Gerald Ford. Second, it stymied commercial agreements that Nixon had reached with the Soviet Union by enacting the Jackson-Vanik Amendment, which tied increased trade with the Soviet Union to its freedom of emigration.

A year later, Congress gave itself greater influence over U.S. arms sales by enacting an amendment to the Arms Export Control Act requiring that major sales of military equipment be subject to congressional disapproval. Additionally, in 1975–76, Senator Frank Church and Representative Otis Pike led prominent congressional committees that investigated CIA abuses and mistakes. As a result of these high-profile investigations, Congress gained new oversight of the intelligence community and greater access to intelligence information.

This new congressional assertiveness, which I generally supported, did not give Congress the upper hand in foreign policy. But it did indicate that Congress was playing an increasingly important role. President Jimmy Carter realized that Congress could no longer be expected to rubber-stamp his policies when he devoted substantial time and energy to consult with Congress to gain its approval of the Panama Canal treaties and arms sales to Saudi Arabia, two extremely controversial issues in Congress.

President Ronald Reagan regained some presidential authority during the 1980s because he was viewed by the American people as a strong leader with a clear vision of the world and a staunch position against communism. But he faced serious congressional challenges as well, particularly on U.S. policy toward Central America. Congress, with my support, refused on multiple occasions to approve his requests to fund the Contras in Nicaragua—resistance that led his administration to subvert the law in order to provide the aid anyway.

Following the end of the Cold War in 1989, foreign policy relations between Congress and the president were frequently rocky. President George H. W. Bush managed to win congressional support for the Gulf War after an intensive five-month lobbying campaign on Capitol Hill. But President Bill Clinton struggled mightily, and sometimes unsuccessfully, to gain congressional approval for a variety of foreign policy initiatives, from the Comprehensive Test Ban Treaty and fast-track authority for trade agreements to funding for the United Nations, the International Monetary Fund, international peacekeeping, and foreign aid. Executive–legislative relations reached another low point with President Clinton's impeachment, which exacerbated the mutual mistrust between Congress and the president and made foreign policy cooperation between the branches increasingly rare during Clinton's second term.

Foreign policy debates remained acrimonious during the early months of George W. Bush's presidency, but Congress rallied around him following the terrorist attacks in September 2001, quickly authorizing the use of force against al Qaeda and appropriating large increases in funding for homeland security, intelligence, and defense. The war on terrorism may trigger an increase in presidential power, particularly if there are additional major attacks on the United States. However, it is unlikely that Congress will give up its hard-won foreign policy influence.

The Evolving International Environment

Congress's assertiveness in recent decades has been heavily influenced by the evolving international environment. During the Cold War, particularly until the Vietnam conflict, the president commanded great authority, in large part because Americans felt a strong collective threat to their national security. Members of Congress who challenged the president could be charged with lacking patriotism and undermining the national interest. That political environment encouraged members to fall in line behind the president.

In the decade after the end of the Cold War, most Americans felt more secure and paid less attention to international events. Instead of facing the dominant threat of communism, the nation confronted a more complex and diverse set of international challenges. During the 1990s, the world was transformed by revolutions in information and communications technology, while new security threats and issues such as human rights and global warming increasingly took center stage.

The September 2001 terrorist attacks brought us into a new era, showing us that we were not as secure as we believed ourselves to be. For the first time since the Gulf War ten years earlier, the nation was galvanized by world events and determined to defeat an adversary. In the wake of the terrorist attacks, the power of the presidency returned, at least temporarily, to its Cold War heights—though it is too early to determine the long-term impact of the war on terrorism on executive–legislative relations.

America's international preeminence today gives it some distinct advantages in the pursuit of its foreign policy goals. For instance, only it can project military power anywhere in the world. Yet in many respects the formulation and conduct of foreign policy today are more complex and difficult than ever before. Security threats are more diffuse, and economic and financial issues have greater prominence. Instead of facing one superpower with thousands of nuclear weapons, we confront complex threats from states and nonstate actors, including international terrorists; proliferating nuclear, chemical, and biological weapons; information warfare; and the international drug trade and organized crime. Because our economy is increasingly linked to the global economy, we must also focus on issues such as international trade, the health of foreign banking systems, and the regulation of Internet commerce.

Additionally, the U.S. national interest in a particular country or issue is now harder to define than it was during the Cold War. Though issues that have gained a new prominence—advancing democracy and the rule of law, protecting the environment, promoting human rights— are all important, they are not always related directly to vital national interests.

In some nations, we have so many national interests that some can conflict with others. For instance, in congressional debates on trade with China during the 1990s, some members of Congress argued that our national interest in economic growth and peace in Asia compelled us to work to increase trade with China. Other members argued that our national interest in advancing democracy and human rights required that we condition trade with China on Chinese progress in those areas. When the U.S. national interest is unclear or extremely complex, there is often a lack of consensus on what policy should be, which makes it difficult for the president to rally congressional support and encourages members of Congress to advocate various proposals of their own.

More Foreign Policy Actors

In addition to the evolving international environment, a major change of recent years has been the dramatic increase in the number of actors influencing U.S. foreign policy. During the 1950s and 1960s, foreign policy was largely the domain of a small group of people: the president, the secretaries of state and defense, the director of the CIA, the national security advisor, the chairs of the House and Senate foreign affairs committees, and other members of the elite foreign policy establishment. To consult with Congress, the president and his advisors simply needed to call up the key congressional leaders. Today, power in Congress is more widely distributed, so consultation involves talking with many members. Every member takes an interest in foreign policy at one time or another, and every member wants to be heard.

There are also many more groups outside of government seeking to influence foreign policy today: the business community, labor unions, ethnic constituencies, nonprofit organizations, foreign countries, former officials, international organizations, universities, think tanks—and the list goes on. The halls of Congress are filled with representatives of these and other interest groups every day. While serving on the House Foreign Affairs Committee, I spent an enormous amount of time meeting with various groups interested in foreign policy, ranging from pistachio nut growers to associations of religious leaders and heads of state.

The lobbying techniques of interest groups are increasingly sophisticated. Many of them are well organized, have large amounts of money, employ the media effectively, and know how to flood congressional offices with telephone calls, letters, faxes, and e-mail messages. Once I returned to my office after speaking in a committee hearing and found a number of phone messages from constituents in Indiana who were unhappy with some positions I had taken. The hearing had not even been televised, but they had been asked to call my office within minutes by an interest-group representative who had been present at it.

The overall impact of special interests has grown markedly since the end of the Cold War. During the 1990s, the relatively benign international environment and the focus of most Americans on domestic concerns produced a political vacuum that was frequently filled by interest groups. The absence of a single, coherent foreign policy doctrine, such as containment, also left greater room for interest groups to argue that their positions were in the U.S. national interest, as they defined it. The end of the Cold War therefore allowed issues that had not been given great attention to come to the fore. For instance, only in recent years have U.S. foreign policy makers been confronted, in part thanks to interest-group pressure, with the issues of HIV/AIDS, global warming, and religious freedom overseas.

The new focus on the war on terrorism following the attacks on the World Trade Center and the Pentagon reduced the influence of some special interests, at least temporarily. For instance, critics of the United Nations were no longer able to prevent Congress from paying an installment of U.S. arrears on U.N. dues once the Bush administration lobbied for its payment on national security grounds, arguing that U.S. arrears made it more difficult for the administration to gain international backing for America's war on terrorism. With a new major threat to U.S. security, policy makers are more likely to focus on the security dimensions of the national interest than on the more parochial concerns of some interest groups. But if the terrorist threat is reduced, special interests might regain any influence they have lost in the current environment.

The number of interest groups involved in foreign policy has risen in recent decades because international affairs affect a growing number of Americans. For instance, the U.S. economy is increasingly dependent on international trade. This means that many businesses—including small companies and even small farmers—have a greater stake in foreign policy. The overall influence of the business community increased during the 1990s as U.S. involvement in the world economy grew. Business lobbyists played a major role in building congressional support for the North American Free Trade Agreement and trade with China, and in influencing President Clinton to ease sanctions against Iran, Libya, and Sudan.

The flip side of this powerful business support for free trade is the frequent opposition to trade agreements voiced by labor and environmental groups, which tend to believe that trade agreements export jobs out of the

United States and weaken environmental standards overseas. Many congressional Democrats share the views of these groups and are therefore reluctant to approve many trade deals. The result is that U.S. trade policy is sometimes determined as much by the relative influence of various special interests, particularly business and labor, as by an objective consideration of the national interest.

Interest groups often increase their power by enlisting the support of other powerful groups that are sympathetic to their cause. For instance, American Jewish groups have courted and gained the support of evangelical Christians and prominent labor organizations for causes related to Israel, and Americans with roots in India have reached out to U.S. businesses to strengthen their support for increasing the number of immigrant visas given to highly skilled technology workers.

Although many special interest groups know how to influence elected officials, many officials also know how to use such groups to their own advantage. Often the tie that binds them is money. Members of Congress, the president, and other politicians use lobbying groups as a source of critical financial contributions, and as a means to reach blocs of voters.

Ethnic groups are very powerful foreign policy actors. Their influence is certainly not new; it dates back to the nation's earliest days. But the number of politically active groups has grown tremendously, and their lobbying techniques have become much more sophisticated. The groups with the most influence are those that are well funded and have large numbers nationally, heavy concentrations in particular areas of the country, or positions of power in society. These groups have an especially large influence on Congress because a member with a large concentration of a particular group in his or her district has a great incentive to promote foreign policies advocated by that group.

Ethnic congressional caucuses now abound. In the House, there is an Indian Caucus, an Armenian Caucus, an Albanian Caucus, and many more. These caucuses often act as fund-raising mechanisms for members who support their objectives. Some members have close personal ties not just to other nations but to particular political parties in other countries. I was one of a few members who did not join any ethnic caucuses—because, with so many of them, I decided that it would be difficult to join some and refrain from joining others.

Cuban Americans have long had a tremendous impact on U.S. policy toward Cuba because of their concentration in South Florida and a few other areas. They have successfully pushed Republican and Democratic elected officials to maintain and strengthen the U.S. embargo on Cuba during the past four decades. Jewish Americans have had great influence on U.S. policy toward the Middle East, encouraging close ties to Israel and sanctions on Iran, Iraq, and Libya. Supporters of Israel represent one of the most influential lobbying groups in Washington.

Some ethnic groups can exert great influence because of their ties to individual powerful members of Congress. For instance, in a conversation about a foreign aid bill, then–Speaker of the House Tip O'Neill, who represented a Massachusetts district with a large Irish American constituency, told me, "Lee, I'll support whatever legislation you draw up, but make sure it includes aid to Ireland." Given his position of power, there was no doubt that aid for the Irish would be included in that bill.

Many ethnic groups that had little influence a few decades ago now have substantial impact. Consider the rising power of Armenian Americans. Fifteen years ago, Armenia was of little concern to most members of Congress. But thanks to the concentration of Armenian Americans in four major states—California, Massachusetts, New Jersey, and New York—the community has rapidly and dramatically bolstered its influence in national politics.

Following the breakup of the Soviet Union, Armenia and its neighbor Azerbaijan became independent states and fought bitterly over the contested territory of Nagorno-Karabakh, which was part of Azerbaijan at the time. Armenian Americans encouraged Congress to provide substantial aid to Armenia and to cut off U.S. assistance to Azerbaijan. Their strong lobbying resulted in generous aid packages for Armenia and sanctions, enacted in 1992, that prohibited most forms of aid to Azerbaijan. Between 1992 and 2001, Congress approved more than $1 billion in aid for Armenia, making it the second largest recipient of U.S. aid per capita in the world after Israel. Azerbaijan has received much less assistance, though the U.S. sanctions have been eased in recent years, and were temporarily waived in December 2001 to encourage Azerbaijan to support U.S. anti-terrorism efforts. This unbalanced approach to Armenia and Azerbaijan has made it more difficult for the United States to help broker an end to their conflict, gain access to Azerbaijan's huge oil reserves, and use Azerbaijan's military bases, airspace, and intelligence to wage its campaign in Afghanistan.

The African American community is another increasingly powerful foreign policy actor. It has largely driven U.S. policy toward Haiti and brought more U.S. attention to Africa. Black leaders have played an instrumental role during the past two decades in pushing for sanctions to protest apartheid in South Africa, military intervention to oust the military junta that ruled Haiti, and assistance to help African nations fight the AIDS pandemic. They also encouraged President Clinton to take an unprecedented nine-day trip to Africa in 1998. In 2001, civil rights groups joined forces with religious conservatives in an unusual coalition to encourage President George W. Bush to assist Christians being persecuted in southern Sudan.

Some ethnic lobbying groups enhance their influence through close ties to foreign governments. Foreign embassies in Washington often work in tandem with domestic interest groups to coordinate lobbying efforts. Many lobbyists even represent foreign governments or companies directly. Lobbyists hired by the Taiwanese government, for instance, have drafted congressional resolutions that subsequently have been taken up by Congress. Taiwanese representatives frequently visited my office to lobby for various proposals, and on several occasions they invited members of my staff to travel to Taiwan at no cost. Foreign ambassadors are also regular lobbyists on Capitol Hill; on a given day, any number of them can be seen walking the halls of Congress.

In addition, foreign heads of state are often directly involved in the U.S. foreign policy process. Foreign presidents and prime ministers regularly come to Washington to ask for U.S. help of one kind or another. Many of these representatives meet not just with the president and administration officials but also with members of Congress. Egyptian President Anwar Sadat was one of the first foreign leaders to develop a close relationship with many members; he knew me and numerous others on a first-name basis. Georgian President Edward Shevardnadze is another head of state who has developed close ties to members of Congress—stemming largely from his earlier service as Soviet foreign minister. Georgia would command far less attention in Washington—and receive much less U.S. aid—without his influence.

Sometimes, foreign leaders engage Congress in order to get around, or apply pressure on, an administration. In the early 1970s, during Bangladesh's war of independence from Pakistan, representatives of the emerging Bangladeshi leadership came to Washington to lobby members of Congress and the Nixon administration to recognize Bangladesh and support its independence. They found a more favorable attitude in Congress than in the administration, and their congressional lobbying was instrumental in pushing the United States to recognize the new nation. More recently, since the 1991 Gulf War, Iraqi opposition leaders have gained more support in Congress than in the State Department or CIA to help them overthrow Saddam Hussein. Congress has appropriated tens of millions of dollars to support the Iraqi opposition, but the Clinton and George W. Bush administrations, worried about the potential misuse of funds, have been reluctant to disburse all the money.

U.S. presidents in recent years have employed a variation of this tactic: enlisting foreign leaders to lobby Congress on behalf of their proposals. Czech President

Vaclav Havel strengthened congressional support for expanding the North Atlantic Treaty Organization (NATO) during the mid-1990s; Israeli Prime Ministers Yitzhak Rabin and Shimon Peres helped convince Congress to support aid to the Palestinians following the 1993 Oslo peace accords; and British Prime Minister Margaret Thatcher assured Congress during the 1980s that the United States could do business with Soviet Prime Minister Mikhail Gorbachev.

Perhaps no set of actors has seen its influence grow as rapidly in recent years as the wide range of people representing nongovernmental organizations (NGOs), including public interest groups and private voluntary associations. These groups—ranging from Human Rights Watch to the Christian Coalition—advocate positions, and exert power, on every imaginable international issue. U.S. funding for the United Nations, for instance, was tied down for several years in the 1990s by a peripheral anti-abortion provision that was pushed by right-to-life activists and opposed by family-planning groups. Many NGOs shape the public debate on issues of concern to them through grassroots activities and op-ed essays in newspapers nationwide.

Universities and think tanks also play a growing role in the policy debate. Schools of international affairs do not only educate the next generation of foreign policy makers; they participate in the policy-making process themselves by holding conferences and producing books on major international issues. Research institutes, such as the Brookings Institution and the Center for Strategic and International Studies, have proliferated and become increasingly influential in Washington policy debates. I relied heavily on policy briefs and reports produced by these and other think tanks to keep myself informed on international issues and develop policy proposals. Many university professors and think tank experts serve as helpful resources for policy makers.

International organizations also have greater influence today. Thirty years ago, few members of Congress could even name the top officials of major international institutions. Now the leaders of the United Nations, International Monetary Fund, World Bank, and World Trade Organization are in constant contact with U.S. officials and members of Congress. U.S. foreign policy makers often work in consultation with policy makers from these institutions. For instance, the U.S. Treasury Department and the International Monetary Fund frequently cooperate closely to design bailout packages for struggling economies overseas.

Former U.S. officials constitute another increasingly visible group of foreign policy activists. The American people heard little from former Secretaries of State Dean Rusk and William Rogers in the 1960s and 1970s. But today former top officials, such as Henry Kissinger, Brent Scowcroft, James Baker, and Madeleine Albright, remain highly visible on the foreign policy scene. Their voices continue to be heard, even though they left office long ago.

Even states and localities are getting more involved in foreign affairs. Some have enacted sanctions prohibiting trade with certain countries. The Massachusetts legislature, for instance, passed a law during the 1990s that prohibited the state from buying goods from any corporate entity doing business with Burma, in order to protest human rights violations by Burma's military regime. The Supreme Court struck down the law on the grounds that it was preempted by congressional legislation imposing different federal sanctions on the country.

And then there is the media—an increasingly powerful foreign policy actor. Television in particular has the ability to set our foreign policy agenda through the impact of its images. In 1992, television images of starving children in Somalia touched American hearts and led President George H. W. Bush to send U.S. troops to Somalia to help combat its famine. But some months later, television images of dead U.S. soldiers being dragged through the streets of Mogadishu angered Americans and led President Clinton to withdraw our troops just as quickly. More recently, the horrific images of the World Trade Center collapsing fueled American outrage and fostered strong public support for a military response.

The media also tends to hamstring careful deliberation by placing a high premium on quick reactions. Frequently, reporters asked me to state my opinion on a fast-breaking news story before I had the time to develop an informed view on it. Sometimes I spent the better part of my day responding to media inquiries, leaving me little time to consider the implications of certain policies or legislation. The proliferation of media outlets also complicates the president's job because he must compete with so many other voices for the nation's attention.

Changes in Congress

Changes in the institution and practices of Congress have also altered the foreign policy influence of Congress and the president in recent decades. Since the Vietnam War, the foreign policy capacity of Congress has grown both more expert and more diffuse. Greater diversity in Congress, the intensification of the political environment, and the explosion of 24-hour news and information have led Congress to challenge the president more often but frequently in a haphazard, poorly coordinated manner. Congress has become more representative of widely varying American viewpoints, but it has also become more chaotic and divided.

Congress's foreign policy activities have been transformed by the growing individualism and diversity of its members. After the bombing of Pearl Harbor and the resounding U.S. success in World War II, a generation of members of Congress tended to defer to the president and congressional leadership on foreign affairs. But after the tragic failures of Vietnam, many new members, like myself, felt that we should become more involved in foreign policy formulation.

Beginning in the late 1960s, members hired larger and more professional staffs—both in their own offices and on committees. The professional staff of the House Foreign Affairs Committee, for instance, grew from nine people in 1965 to seventy-two in 2001, while that of the Senate Foreign Relations Committee increased from nine to thirty-six during the same period. In my early years in Congress, the principal advisors to the chairman of the House Foreign Affairs Committee were former precinct workers from his district. Today, committee staff members are experts in their fields, often with advanced degrees from the nation's top law schools and universities. I depended on them tremendously for policy analysis and recommendations.

Congress has also strengthened its foreign policy capacity by gaining access to more executive branch documents and sources, including intelligence information, and by greatly expanding its own independent research bodies, such as the Congressional Research Service, the General Accounting Office, and the Congressional Budget Office. This increased access to information and expertise has enabled Congress to get involved in many more aspects of foreign policy, sometimes with as much knowledge as the president.

The greater diversity and wide-ranging experience of today's members of Congress have strengthened their independence. Many newly elected members today have previous experience overseas—be it service in the Peace Corps, work for multinational corporations, or participation in international exchanges. Congress also includes many more women, African Americans, Latinos, and members who are from other ethnic groups than it did just a few decades ago. These members have brought new concerns to the foreign policy debate. The sanctions placed by Congress on South Africa to protest apartheid in the 1980s and the increased national focus on women's rights overseas have reflected the growing power of black and female members. During the 1999 Kosovo War, two Serbian American members brought a special personal perspective to their efforts to seek a peaceful resolution.

Many members today have weaker personal ties to their parties and to the institution of Congress. This makes them more willing to speak out and advance policies on issues of particular concern to them or their constituents. In 2000, for example, an influential senator used his power as chair of a Senate appropriations sub-committee to block hundreds of millions of dollars that had been approved by Congress for U.N. peacekeeping missions because he opposed the administration's policy on Sierra Leone.

Increased polarization and incivility in Congress have often made it all the more difficult for Congress to speak with one voice. In the years following World War II, a powerful bipartisan, centrist contingent of members of Congress shared a similar internationalist outlook and often voted together on key foreign policy issues. Many members also formed close personal relationships with members from the other party. Early in my career, I once made a parliamentary mistake on the floor of the House, and a senior Republican (and good friend) came over and gently pointed out my mistake and how to correct it—and this was on an issue on which we disagreed. I can't imagine that happening today.

Following the tumultuous 1960s, the Democratic Caucus became more liberal while the Republican Caucus grew more conservative. This ideological divergence was accompanied by decreasing bipartisan cooperation and more bickering. Foreign policy issues were increasingly used by members to further their domestic political interests, often by attacking their opponents, rather than to advance the national interest. The media's often negative, cynical, and adversarial coverage of politics has helped to fuel the growing incivility in Congress. The politicians who scream the loudest tend to get the most media coverage. Members of Congress with moderate views are often rejected by news analysis programs because producers believe they will not attract many viewers.

The policy-making process has been further complicated by internal splits within the political parties on
many foreign policy issues. On trade policy, for instance,
pro-trade Republicans and Democrats are often allied
against members of both parties who want the United
States to take stronger stances on labor standards, human rights, religious freedom, national security, or the
environment. During the 1990s, more Republican than
Democratic members of Congress voted with President
Clinton on several key trade promotion issues, such as
extending most-favored-nation trading status to China.
Developing a unified position on a foreign policy issue in
Congress has become extremely difficult, and on a controversial issue it can be virtually impossible.

This fragmentation of Congress is heightened by the
more frequent turnover of members today. Membership
in Congress used to be considered a lifetime career, but
now many people join the institution for just a few
years. This greater transience brings many fresh voices
into Congress, but it also reduces the number of members with a memory of history and a long-term perspective on foreign policy matters. New members are often
confronted with important foreign policy issues for the
first time when they enter Congress. They react to them
in all kinds of ways.

These and other changes in Congress have fueled a
large-scale diffusion of power in the institution. Foreign
policy influence is now spread in a confusing manner
among dozens of committees, from Agriculture, to Banking, to Government Affairs, rather than being concen-
trated in the main foreign policy committees, which have
traditionally contained the greatest foreign policy expertise. Power is diffused further through the growing ten-

dency to form ad hoc caucuses on issues such as trade, terrorism, or the environment. This fragmentation of power has made it all the more difficult for Congress to develop a foreign policy consensus.

With the absence of a centralized forum for the debate and passage of foreign affairs legislation, Congress addresses many international issues in isolation by passing independent foreign policy measures or tacking amendments onto other bills that are not related directly to international affairs. When Congress uses these legislative techniques, it sidesteps the traditional refining process of committee hearings, deliberations, and votes. It thereby shortcuts deliberation and fails to use much of its foreign policy expertise.

The greatest concentration of foreign policy power in Congress resides now in the appropriations committees, in which international concerns are usually secondary to domestic political and fiscal concerns. The dominance of the appropriations committees was felt throughout the 1990s as Congress continually cut international affairs funding from the amounts requested by President Clinton, preferring to devote money to more popular tax cuts or domestic programs.

It has become common to bring foreign policy bills directly to the House and Senate floors without full consideration by the foreign policy committees. Remarkably, the foreign affairs committees have not passed comprehensive authorizing legislation for the U.S. foreign assistance budget since 1985—because committee members want to avoid making decisions on every tough foreign policy issue, and administrations want to prevent the passage of restrictive riders that often get attached to authorizing legislation. Instead, important foreign policy issues are now frequently decided in enormous omnibus bills worked out in secret, late-night negotiations among a limited group of congressional leaders and White House and congressional staffs. In 1998, for instance, the appropriations omnibus bill, totaling about $500 billion, included such key foreign policy issues as implementing legislation for the Chemical Weapons Convention and supplemental funding for the International Monetary Fund and peacekeeping operations in Bosnia. These omnibus bills—often gauged more by weight than the number of pages—are abominations. No member of Congress has a chance to read much of them, let alone understand them, before they are voted on. Their increasing prevalence has led many observers to question whether authorizing committees are still needed at all.

Congressional responsibility has been further weakened in recent decades by the growing influence of domestic political concerns on the foreign policy process. Politics has certainly always played a role in foreign policy, but its influence became greater during the 1980s and 1990s. Many of today's members of Congress view foreign policy as nothing more than an extension of local or national politics. They use foreign policy to curry favor with supporters or constituents, or to score political points by attacking the president.

Some Republicans in Congress placed politics before sound policy during the Clinton years by calling the president's policies toward China, Iraq, and North Korea appeasement without offering any constructive alternatives. Some Democrats have attempted to advance their own political interests by opposing the passage of trade promotion authority for the president—a position favored by key supporters of the Democrats, particularly labor unions. The bipartisan political support for President George W. Bush in the difficult weeks after the September 2001 terrorist attacks was a refreshing exception to this trend.

The rise of the perpetual political campaign has rendered the congressional foreign policy capacity even thinner because members now spend so much time campaigning and fund raising that insufficient time is left for careful policy deliberation. Even when members are focused on policy, international affairs are usually, though not always, at the bottom of their list of concerns. Most members seek to join committees, such as Appropriations, Banking, and Commerce, that are more financially and politically lucrative than the foreign affairs committees.

The result of all of these changes in Congress since the 1960s is a more representative, assertive, diffuse, and inconsistent congressional role in foreign policy. Congress challenges the president's authority far more often today than it did four decades ago, but it sometimes acts haphazardly or rashly and speaks in a cacophony of conflicting voices.

Changes in the Executive Branch

Some of these changes in the way Congress approaches and handles foreign policy have been mirrored in the executive branch. Foreign policy authority in the executive has also become more diffuse, as the number of federal agencies involved in it has proliferated. The State Department, Defense Department, and CIA remain the central bodies for much of foreign policy, but they are no longer the exclusive authorities. The Treasury Department, for instance, now handles most international economic issues. The Justice Department manages immigration policy and the war on drugs, and it is heavily involved, through the Federal Bureau of Investigation, in counterterrorism efforts. The Departments of Energy, Commerce, and Agriculture, as well as the Office of the U.S. Trade Representative, play important foreign policy roles as well. Additionally, within the Defense Department, regional commanders of U.S. forces have increasing influence because they control the U.S. military assets that are deployed in the field. It is not unusual for the various executive agencies to compete and collide on foreign policy issues.

The diffusion of executive authority is fueled by the changing, and increasingly complex, agenda of foreign policy. The Departments of State and Defense are best suited to manage diplomatic and security issues, but today's agenda is full of technical and scientific problems—ranging from international finance, to AIDS, to the global environment—that require other kinds of expertise. The Gore-Chernomyrdin Commission, which was established during the Clinton presidency to help manage U.S.–Russian relations, reflected this need for specialized knowledge and input. It matched up U.S. and Russian experts from outside the traditional foreign policy apparatus to discuss issues such as health, energy, and the environment.

Along with the general diffusion of foreign policy authority has come a greater concentration of power in the National Security Council (NSC). The NSC is the primary manager and coordinator of the various foreign

policy activities conducted by the executive departments. Because many people are involved in executive
branch policy making, it can be difficult for an administration to speak with one voice. During George W.
Bush's presidency, for instance, conflicting statements
by Secretary of Defense Donald Rumsfeld and Secretary
of State Colin Powell on some issues, such as whether to
conduct negotiations with North Korea, have created
uncertainty about administration policies. It is the job
of the NSC's head, the national security advisor, to keep
the administration on a single track.

The NSC has evolved since the 1960s into a policy-
making, as well as policy-coordinating, body. Recent
presidents have given the NSC substantial authority for
the development and execution of foreign and security
policy. In many ways, the NSC now resembles a government agency more than a presidential staff. It has
its own policy, legislative, communication, and speech-
making divisions that enable it to interact in many ways
with Congress, the media, the American people, and foreign governments.

Why has the NSC taken on more foreign policy responsibilities? The growing complexity of international
issues, the weakening of the State Department, the need
to manage the interagency process, the national security
advisor's proximity to the president, and the politicization of many aspects of foreign policy have all contributed to the trend. Because foreign policy issues now
involve many dimensions, from finance to the environment, it has become harder for any single department,
such as State or Defense, to handle an issue comprehen-
sively. Foreign aid programs, for instance, are no longer

run mainly by the State Department but rather are dispersed among several government agencies. The NSC has therefore adopted more responsibility for managing them. The underfunding of the State Department during the past decade has further weakened its capacity to take the lead on foreign policy issues.

The influence of the NSC has been enhanced by the increased importance of instantaneous communication. Unlike the secretaries of state and defense, the national security advisor, with an office in the White House, is almost always within walking distance of the president. When the president wants a quick opinion or briefing on a breaking foreign policy issue, he is likely to turn to the person who can be in his office within seconds. The influence of President George W. Bush's national security advisor, Condoleezza Rice, was evident when she accompanied Bush on his one-month "working vacation" in August 2001, living in a trailer on his Texas ranch.

The politicization of the foreign-policy-making process has further boosted the influence of the NSC. Every issue—from trade to energy policy—is now subject to intense scrutiny based on political, and sometimes partisan, concerns. Those concerns enter into executive branch decision making most often in the White House. President Clinton, for instance, emphasized foreign policy issues such as NATO expansion, sanctions on Cuba, and the pursuit of peace in Northern Ireland in part because they would help him earn votes from major ethnic groups. President George W. Bush has hoped to increase his appeal among Hispanic voters by reaching out to Mexico, and he has sought greater support in steel-producing states by placing tariffs on steel imports.

Another change in the executive branch is in the role played by U.S. diplomats. Globalization and the proliferation of new threats to U.S. security have placed new burdens upon them. The traditional responsibilities of diplomacy, such as negotiating treaties, managing alliances and relations with adversaries, and supporting U.S. businesses overseas, are still critical elements of diplomatic work. But today diplomats must also deal with the heavy demands generated by instantaneous communications and the growing, increasingly complex agenda of international issues—which range from trade rules and telecommunications standards to drug trafficking and the proliferation of weapons of mass destruction. An ambassador to Paris or Berlin, for instance, now needs to be up-to-date on genetically engineered crops, climate change, monetary union within the European Union, and numerous other issues.

The demands placed on U.S. posts have also changed. A primary function of our overseas embassies has traditionally been to collect and report information on foreign trends and events. This function is still important, but it is not as important as it once was because more news and information is available to policy makers through other outlets, such as the media. U.S. posts must now spend more time dealing with trade, the environment, and other complex global issues such as terrorism. They are staffed by experts in these issues from many U.S. agencies, from the Department of Agriculture to the CIA. More than thirty U.S. agencies are now represented among the 14,000 Americans posted in embassies, consulates, and missions overseas.

While handling their increasingly complex load, our overseas posts must respond to an ever-growing number of instructions from Washington. Diplomats may be instructed to lobby a foreign government, attend local social functions, or even deliver sensitive mail. At the same time, most American diplomats today complain that Washington often bypasses them in making important foreign policy decisions. They are also burdened with an increasing number of requests for assistance from U.S. businesses and citizens, as the U.S. private sector becomes more engaged internationally and more Americans travel and live overseas.

A serious problem confronting the executive branch today is its difficulty recruiting and retaining top-flight diplomats and foreign policy specialists. During the Cold War, working on foreign policy or national security issues for the government was appealing to many people and, for some, even prestigious. As the salience of international issues diminished during the 1990s in the minds of Americans, and exciting and far more lucrative opportunities opened up in the private sector, careers in foreign policy became less attractive. Family considerations, such as the difficulty of moving a two-career family overseas, have further restricted the appeal of diplomatic service. For these and other reasons, increasing numbers of talented people have left government service and fewer young people have sought to join the government ranks. Between 1994 and 2000, resignations by Foreign Service specialists in the State Department quadrupled, creating by 2001 a deficit of some 1,100 Foreign Service and Civil Service officers.

Because many graduates of public affairs schools now choose to work in the private sector, those vacancies have become harder to fill. Whereas three-quarters of young Americans graduating from Harvard's prestigious Kennedy School of Government went on to work for the government in 1980, that proportion was down to one-third in 2001. Following the terrorist attacks on New York and Washington, however, there were signs of a renewed interest among young people in foreign affairs careers, as more than three times the normal number of applicants took the Foreign Service examination. So there is hope that the institutions of U.S. foreign policy will soon again attract the best and the brightest.

All of these changes of recent years in the international environment, U.S. domestic politics, and Congress and the presidency have produced a more representative, contentious, and erratic foreign policy process. Foreign policy has changed from being the domain of a select few to being an activity involving many thousands of Americans and innumerable policy makers. It is now more representative of the diverse views of the American people and more accountable to the public. Like many other aspects of American life, it is also more fast paced, more media driven, and more centered on short-term concerns than it was four decades ago. This makes the task of achieving a consensus on the formulation and conduct of U.S. foreign policy—for both the president and Congress—all the more difficult.

CHAPTER 3

Continuities in the Making of Foreign Policy

Although many elements of the foreign policy process have changed since the 1960s, much has remained the same. Presidential leadership, congressional partnership and oversight, and sustained consultation between the branches are still the essential ingredients for a successful foreign policy. For the United States to advance and protect its interests around the world, the president and Congress must work together to craft a bipartisan foreign policy that is supported by the American people.

The Role of the President

The president remains the most important foreign policy maker. Only he is accountable to, and speaks for, all Americans, and only he can rally public or international support to a foreign policy cause. The president's command of the bully pulpit gives him an unrivaled power to influence the foreign policy debate. When he vigorously takes his case on a major foreign policy issue to Congress and the American people, he usually wins their support.

Moreover, though Congress plays an important role in formulating foreign policy, the president is responsible for its implementation. The president directs our nation's diplomats, intelligence agencies, and armed services, and he negotiates with foreign leaders. He has the primary responsibility for making foreign policy work. The United States can achieve little internationally without strong presidential leadership.

On rare occasions in recent decades, Congress has taken the lead on foreign policy, but most actions have followed a proposal by the president. Consider the major foreign policy initiatives of the past sixty years. The president played the central role in nearly all of them:

- Franklin Roosevelt rallied the country to fight and win World War II and began developing important postwar institutions, such as the United Nations, the International Monetary Fund, and the World Bank.
- Harry Truman mobilized Americans for the Cold War battle against communism and championed the Marshall Plan to rebuild Europe and the critical NATO security alliance.
- Dwight Eisenhower negotiated the cease-fire that ended the Korean War.
- John Kennedy brought the nation back from the brink of nuclear war by resolving the Cuban missile crisis.
- Lyndon Johnson escalated U.S. military intervention in Vietnam in order to contain communism.

- Richard Nixon overcame years of mistrust to renew U.S. relations with China.
- Jimmy Carter negotiated the Panama Canal treaties and the Camp David accords establishing peace between Israel and Egypt.
- Ronald Reagan intensified the U.S. challenge to the Soviet Union and started deep cuts in nuclear weapons.
- George H. W. Bush skillfully managed the end of the Cold War and built the coalition that forced Iraq out of Kuwait.
- Bill Clinton strengthened and expanded NATO, advanced free trade, and helped secure nuclear weapons facilities in Russia.
- George W. Bush rallied the nation and the world to root out al Qaeda and combat international terrorism.

What must the president do to be an effective leader in foreign policy? Most important, he must make foreign policy a priority. Any president faces immense pressures to focus on the domestic agenda, but success in foreign policy demands substantial time and energy. When the president concentrates his energy and the nation's attention on an international problem, the United States usually achieves success. But too frequently—although often for compelling reasons, given the many demands of the job—the president's attention (as well as the attention of the American people) moves away from a problem once the guns go silent but before a full solution has been achieved. This has been the case, for instance, in Haiti, Bosnia, Kosovo, and Afghanistan, where the United States expended substantial energy and resources to end repressive or conflict-ridden situations but has been reluctant to provide sufficient leadership and funding in the aftermath to maintain stability and foster lasting peace. Because of the constant press of many world crises demanding U.S. leadership, sustaining policy over time can be extremely difficult. Only the president can do it.

The president must also decide which foreign policy issues to focus on. Faced with a long list of international challenges, he must determine which critical issues deserve his attention and leadership. He must keep his eye on the big picture and not let issues of secondary importance consume too much of his time. The most important issues for U.S. foreign policy are protecting national security, advancing international prosperity, and strengthening relations with other world powers, particularly Europe, Japan, China, and Russia. These issues must be at the center of the president's foreign policy.

The president must know where he wants to go and how he intends to get there. He must set firm goals so his policy is driven not by day-to-day events but by a broad strategic vision. He must then explain his goals to the American people, members of Congress, and other nations; articulate his policy proposals clearly; and specify what kinds of resources he wants to expend on them. His goals and proposals give crucial guidance to his entire administration and to Congress.

Often, presidents are reluctant to articulate foreign policy in detail and with precision—because policy articulation is hard to do and requires a lot of preparation. The writing of a single foreign policy speech can require the president and his advisors to make dozens of policy decisions. This process can be extremely time consuming and contentious. But a reluctance to articulate policy with precision is usually a mistake. Though deliberate ambiguity can sometimes be desirable, as in the case of articulating the precise U.S. response should war break out between China and Taiwan, it does not usually serve American interests.

A lack of clarity in policy frequently creates confusion, both down the line in the administration and among foreign governments. Some policy makers have observed that it is difficult enough to go on the Sunday morning talk shows to explain and defend policies that are known; imagine how difficult it is for them to defend a policy they do not fully understand because the president has not made it clear. Policy clarity can also influence the most serious developments of war and peace. For instance, if Iraqi President Saddam Hussein had known that George H. W. Bush would retaliate militarily against an Iraqi invasion of Kuwait, he might not have ordered the invasion in 1990. A clearer articulation of the president's support for Kuwait might therefore have prevented the subsequent war. By contrast, clear articulation of policy did help keep the Gulf War within certain limits. Bush's warning that the United States would retaliate harshly against any Iraqi use of weapons of mass destruction discouraged Hussein from employing them against U.S. troops or Israel.

A major challenge for the president is explaining the international environment and U.S. national interests to members of Congress and the American people. Public and congressional support for the president's initiatives comes only if Americans understand the issues and challenges we confront. This task of educating the American people about foreign policy is especially difficult for a president today because many other voices—on television, radio, and the Internet—compete for the public's attention. To be heard above the clamor, the president must begin to educate the American people at the outset of his term and keep at it until his final day in office. This cannot be done solely in interviews and press conferences. Presidential speeches on foreign policy are essential.

The president also must work in close partnership with friendly leaders around the world. Strong personal relationships between the president and foreign heads of state help build international backing for U.S. policies. These relationships are critical because we need international cooperation and support to meet most foreign policy challenges, from terrorism to global warming. All presidents recognize the importance of developing these relationships and place a high priority on cultivating them. President George W. Bush, for instance, has sought to establish a good rapport with Mexican President Vicente Fox and Russian President Vladimir Putin in order to put U.S. relations with Mexico and Russia on a stronger footing and gain backing for U.S. policies on issues including hemispheric free trade, ballistic missile defense, and terrorism.

Finally, the president must work with Congress to develop a bipartisan approach to the major foreign policy challenges. Few words in politics are as bandied about, and paid as much lip service, as bipartisanship. All politicians recognize that, like freedom or prosperity, its approval ratings approach 100 percent. Yet translating rhetorical support for bipartisanship into practice can be extremely difficult. The president usually defines bipartisanship as members of the opposing party following his lead. In recent years, the nation's politics have been especially partisan, and U.S. foreign policy has suffered as a result.

Foreign policy always has more force to it when the president and Congress speak with one voice. When the president works with Congress and the opposing party and takes their views into consideration, the policy that results is more likely to have strong public support. And foreign policy with strong domestic support makes the United States more respected and effective abroad.

Foreign Policy Principles and Goals

To foster bipartisanship, the president should work with Congress to build upon the areas of broad agreement in U.S. foreign policy. Despite significant disagreements over tactics, there is a substantial national consensus on several central foreign policy principles and objectives. The president should work to solidify and expand public support and congressional coalitions around these core principles and goals. From that solid base, he can branch out to gain backing for his policies on more specific or controversial issues.

The fundamental principle that should guide the president's approach to foreign policy is that U.S. engagement and leadership are essential to promote American national interests. Most Americans recognize that the United States has a special responsibility and opportunity to make the world a better and safer place—by marshaling the forces of peace and progress, combating international terrorism, extending the benefits of the global economy, and strengthening democratic ideals and practices. At the same time, the president must be sensitive to the limits of our involvement. Our engagement must be selective, closely tied to our interests and opportunities.

The president should also recognize that we must strike the right balance between leadership and partnership. If we attempt to impose our policies on other nations, we risk stirring up a backlash against us. So the challenge for U.S. leadership is to use America's power to develop an international consensus that is consistent with American values and objectives. The president should follow the sound instincts of Americans, who generally prefer multilateral efforts to unilateral ones by overwhelming margins.

Although we must be willing to act alone when our interests demand it, we should strongly support allies and international institutions that help us bear the burdens of leadership. If we do not consistently engage our allies, we may be blissfully free, but we will also be alone and ineffective. America's genius during the past half-century has been in building international institutions—such as the United Nations, the International Monetary Fund, and NATO—that advance U.S. interests through multilateral cooperation. We must lead multilaterally whenever we can, and unilaterally only when we must.

The president and Congress should focus on America's four most important relationships—those with Europe, Japan, China, and Russia. This is exceedingly hard to do, because foreign policy crises constantly pop up and distract the president. Yet much of what we want to achieve in the world requires cooperation with other major powers. The president and Congress should keep our alliances with Europe and Japan—our most important international partnerships—at the center of our foreign policy, and should seek to build more constructive relations with our former adversaries, Russia and China. Our goal should be to encourage positive change in Russia and China by integrating them more deeply into the international community.

There is strong support among Americans for modernizing and strengthening the world's preeminent military. We should also adapt it to take on new challenges, such as homeland defense and international peacekeeping. In the economic sphere, the president should build upon the broad public support for U.S. leadership in promoting international prosperity. He should pursue expanded open trade in conjunction with policies, such as development assistance, that seek to close the yawning worldwide gap between the rich and poor.

The president should also use his political influence to prevent and resolve conflicts overseas, from South Asia and the Korean peninsula to Colombia and the Middle East. In some cases, only the United States has the standing and influence to effectively facilitate peace talks.

While pursuing these broad objectives, the president and Congress should keep American foreign policy firmly embedded in the values that are a great source of U.S. strength: freedom, equality of opportunity, tolerance, pluralism, the rule of law, and shared responsibility. Americans believe deeply in these fundamental ideals, and people around the world look to the United States to protect them when they are under threat. We have a responsibility for and an important interest in ensuring that they continue to spread, rather than recede. Democracies and nations that respect human rights are less likely to go to war, less likely to traffic in terrorism, and more likely to stand against the forces of hatred, intolerance, and destruction.

If the president takes charge of foreign policy, reaches out to Congress and foreign leaders, and builds on the areas of broad agreement in foreign affairs, he will give himself the best opportunity to craft a bipartisan foreign policy that gains public and international support.

The Contributions of Congress

Without the constructive cooperation of Congress, the president faces severe constraints on what he can achieve. A strong foreign policy requires that Congress live up to its constitutional mandate to be the president's partner in developing policy. Congress should be an independent critic of the president, but that criticism should always aim to improve and strengthen U.S. policy.

The conduct of Congress in foreign policy is often criticized (and I have been a harsh critic of it on many occasions), but to its credit Congress has a relatively good record on foreign policy overall. On many issues, Congress has acted responsibly and left a positive imprint on policy. By and large, it has supported the broad themes of U.S. foreign policy since World War II: internationalism, containment of communism, a strong defense, a military presence in Europe and Asia, free trade, close relations with key allies, the promotion of democracy and human rights, and the war on terrorism. Only rarely has Congress turned down a major presidential initiative in foreign policy.

Following World War II, Congress played a critical role in establishing the United Nations, International Monetary Fund, World Bank, and NATO. After healthy debates on each of these institutions, it supported U.S. membership in all of them. Congress also supported and funded the expensive Marshall Plan to promote economic reconstruction and development in Europe beginning in 1948. In the years since, it has usually, though not always, provided the funding needed by international institutions to continue and expand their operations to meet new challenges.

Congress has also worked well with successive presidents during several decades to promote freer international trade. It has approved nearly every major trade liberalization initiative submitted by presidents, including, in the 1990s, the North American Free Trade Agreement and the Uruguay Round accords establishing the World Trade Organization and broadly liberalizing world trade. Congress's refusal during the Clinton years to renew fast-track authority, which would have made it easier to negotiate trade agreements, was a notable exception to this trend.

One of Congress's most important contributions to U.S. foreign policy has been in encouraging the protection and promotion of human rights. Beginning in the 1970s, Congress helped bring increased attention to human rights violations in the Soviet Union, Eastern Europe, Latin America, and other places. In 1974, with the Jackson-Vanik Amendment, it barred the president from giving favorable trade treatment to nations that restrict free emigration; in 1975, it passed a bill mandating that the executive branch produce reports on human rights for the first time; and in 1977, it established the position of assistant secretary of state for human rights. Thanks in part to these and other congressional actions, and to President Carter's leadership, human rights became a central element of U.S. foreign policy. In the 1980s, Congress helped to promote human rights in South Africa by enacting sanctions on the country to protest apartheid— over President Reagan's opposition.

In addition, Congress has protected U.S. security by crafting and funding the important Cooperative Threat Reduction Program, which has provided critical assistance during the past decade for dismantling nuclear, chemical, and other weapons in the former Soviet Union. With the help of this aid, all nuclear weapons were removed from Ukraine, Kazakhstan, and Belarus during the 1990s, and thousands of Russian-controlled weapons have been made more secure. The Cooperative Threat Reduction Program, which I supported, was largely a congressional initiative, as reflected in its popular title, the Nunn-Lugar Act, after Senators Sam Nunn and Richard Lugar. It was opposed initially by President George H. W. Bush, but subsequently backed by Bush and President Clinton.

Congress has also contributed constructively to foreign policy in recent years by supplying the necessary funding for aid to Israel and other Middle Eastern peace partners; appropriating substantial amounts of money to fight AIDS worldwide; endorsing the enlargement of NATO to include Poland, the Czech Republic, and

Hungary; and providing many billions of dollars and useful recommendations for the fight against international terrorism. So Congress has much to be proud of in foreign policy.

Congressional Strengths

Congress brings many strengths to the foreign policy process. As the most representative branch of government, it reflects like no other institution the diverse views of the American people. Congress can mediate the various perspectives of Americans and help to shape them into a consensual approach. Some of these views may be shortsighted or misguided, but when Congress and the president take them all into consideration in the formulation of foreign policy, the policy that results is more likely to gain the American people's support and to have long-term success.

Congress is the most accessible branch of government. When you wish to convey your views on foreign policy to a policy maker, you cannot call the president or the secretary of state and expect to have your views considered by them. You cannot even reach an assistant secretary of state. But you can call your representative or senator and expect at least to be listened to. This accessibility keeps Congress in touch with the American people and helps ensure that foreign policy is not the exclusive domain of the policy elite.

During my tenure in Congress, I spent countless hours talking to constituents about various foreign policy issues, often one-to-one. When a crisis overseas broke, I would frequently receive numerous phone calls in my office, and would speak directly with as many constituents as I could. They often told me that they were frustrated with their inability to reach policy makers in the executive branch, and I was gratified to be able to address some of their concerns.

Members of Congress also learn a lot from their constituent contacts—even about foreign policy issues. During a meeting I held with a group of constituents in a rural community hall in southern Indiana in the late 1970s, one man stood up and raised the subject of the Panama Canal treaties, which had not yet been heavily discussed in the media. He laid out the clearest, most evenly reasoned argument for ratifying the treaties that I was ever to hear—even after the treaty debate mushroomed into a raging national issue. I was flabbergasted, but took it as a humbling reminder that as a member of Congress you can always find constituents who know more about a given subject than you do.

Congress benefits as well from a wide range of other sources of opinions and expertise. Many members of Congress are knowledgeable on a broad range of foreign policy issues, and a pool of talented congressional staff follows international affairs with great interest and insight. Congress is often more willing than the president to seek input from people outside the government, including from academia, research institutions, and the private sector. I relied on a wide range of sources of information and advice on foreign policy issues. Members of Congress can—and do—call attention to foreign policy concerns that have, for whatever reason, been neglected by the president.

Congress can also usually help to refine and improve policy. The president may not always appreciate having 535 national security advisors, but congressional advice is often constructive and helpful. Because members of Congress do not serve at the president's pleasure, they are in a better position than his aides to offer unvarnished criticism of his policies. The president's foreign policy legislative proposals are frequently strengthened following congressional consideration of them.

Congress can also play a useful role by forcing the president and top administration officials to articulate and explain policy—so the American people and the world can better understand it. Each time the secretary of state, secretary of defense, or another high-ranking official testifies before Congress, the president's policy is conveyed more clearly—not only to Congress but also to other administration officials, to other countries, and, through media reports, to the public at large. In early 2002, as the war on terrorism entered a new phase following the U.S. successes in Afghanistan, leading congressional Democrats asked President Bush to explain his goals for the war's next phase. Their questions forced the administration to articulate its goals more clearly, thereby refining the U.S. approach to the war and keeping the American people informed about its aims.

In addition, Congress can provide crucial backing that strengthens the president's hand in international negotiations. Legislation passed by Congress can indicate to foreign leaders that the president's proposals are backed by the American people. Congressional measures calling for more burden sharing in military deployments, for instance, have helped the president convince

U.S. allies to take on more peacekeeping responsibilities in places like the Balkans.

One of Congress's most underappreciated but important foreign policy roles is oversight. Congress must do more than write the laws; it must make sure that the administration is carrying out those laws the way Congress intended. As President Woodrow Wilson put it: "Quite as important as lawmaking is vigilant oversight of administration." As more power is delegated to the executive and as more laws are passed, the need for oversight grows.

Congressional oversight of foreign policy can help protect the country from the imperial presidency and from bureaucratic arrogance. It can make sure that foreign policy programs conform to congressional intent, are administered efficiently, are not subject to waste and abuse, and remain useful. Congress has a responsibility to look into every nook and cranny of governmental affairs. Through oversight, it can examine everything the government does and expose wrongdoing.

Often, Congress underestimates its oversight power. Agencies start to get a little nervous whenever someone from Congress starts poking around, and that is probably to the good overall. Congressional oversight helps keep federal bureaucracies on their toes.

Congress can use several tools to investigate federal agencies and hold them accountable, including hearings, periodic reauthorization, personal visits by members or their staffs, review by the General Accounting Office (GAO) or inspectors general, subpoenas, and mandated reports or letters from the executive branch.

I found several of these tools useful while serving on the House Foreign Affairs Committee. For instance, I helped to pin down several administrations on their positions on arms sales to Taiwan by pressing them to provide written policy statements, which I subsequently inserted into the *Congressional Record*. During the Clinton administration, I used the same tactic to help clarify the administration's position on the so-called Agreed Framework on North Korea and U.S. policy toward Bosnia. Additionally, the Foreign Affairs Committee kept tabs on foreign assistance projects by mandating State Department reports on the impact of U.S. aid on recipient countries and by authorizing GAO investigations of various foreign aid programs.

Travel overseas was also useful to my committee colleagues, my staff, and me. For example, periodic trips to Bosnia to look into specific aspects of the implementation of the Dayton peace accords enhanced our understanding of the situation on the ground and served notice to the administration that Congress was monitoring U.S. activities in Bosnia. Congressional trips abroad are often criticized as wasteful "junkets," but such trips are essential to allow members of Congress to independently assess U.S. policy. Congressional travel can also help foreign leaders understand the important role Congress plays in the American foreign policy process.

One of the most important foreign policy responsibilities of Congress is to oversee the U.S. intelligence community. Only Congress can provide strong, vigorous, and thorough oversight of the intelligence community that is independent of the executive branch. Unlike most federal agencies, the intelligence community does not receive close scrutiny from any other source. So if Congress fails to identify the problems in intelligence, they are unlikely to be spotted.

Oversight of intelligence is especially important because the intelligence community is very large, complex, and expensive; and because information is power, it has a tremendous ability to influence U.S. policy. Intelligence is an area of temptation for presidents, who can manipulate the policy debate by citing intelligence selectively or encouraging the intelligence community to give them certain types of information. Too often, presidents see intelligence as a tool to make policy look good, rather than as a tool for making good policy. Presidents can also be tempted to resort to the CIA for covert actions when they are frustrated by obstacles to their public policies. Only Congress stands between presidents and the misuse of the intelligence community. Congressional oversight of intelligence is based on the important premise that all government agencies, especially secret ones, require scrutiny by elected officials who are accountable to the American people.

Congressional oversight of the intelligence community is relatively new, but since the Intelligence Oversight Act of 1980 it has been a matter of law. This law requires the executive branch to keep the House and Senate intelligence committees fully and currently informed of intelligence activities, and requires it to report illegal or failed activity in a timely fashion. It also requires all intelligence agencies to furnish the intelligence committees with any information they deem necessary to carry out their responsibilities.

Yet intelligence oversight still does not have a strong legal foundation. There is no comprehensive legal framework for the intelligence community; instead, there is a complex set of laws and executive orders produced during the past six decades. This is a remarkable state of affairs in a country that takes the rule of law so seriously. While serving on the House Intelligence Committee, I tried to create a comprehensive law to govern the intelligence community, but the bill became so long (hundreds of pages), complicated, and contentious that it was dropped.

The very phrase "intelligence community" reflects the community's diffuse and sprawling nature. It includes the CIA, the National Security Agency, the Defense Intelligence Agency, the National Reconnaissance Office, the National Imagery and Mapping Agency, the Federal Bureau of Investigation (for counterterrorism), the intelligence agencies of the Armed Services, and divisions of the State, Energy, and Treasury departments. The director of central intelligence, who also serves as the director of the CIA, is the preeminent intelligence official, but he has limited authority over many of the budgets and programs that he nominally controls. The diffuse nature of the intelligence community is an additional reason for close congressional oversight.

In conducting intelligence oversight, Congress must strike a balance between its need to ensure greater accountability and the intelligence community's need to gather information and protect sources and methods. The purpose of oversight should not be to rein in the intelligence community, though abuses should be uncovered and rooted out. Rather, the basic purpose of oversight should be to ensure that the right people are getting the right information and analysis at the right time. For instance, in the wake of the September 2001 terrorist attacks, it is appropriate for Congress to examine whether the intelligence community properly assembled and disseminated information on the threat posed by al Qaeda in the months and years leading up to the attacks.

Congressional oversight has helped to strengthen the impact of intelligence on policy making over the years by encouraging the intelligence community to devote as much attention to analysis as to the collection of information, and to focus on getting that information and analysis in a timely manner to the policy makers, diplomats, and commanders who need it.

Congressional Deficiencies

In conjunction with these strengths, Congress has many deficiencies in foreign policy. Congress often fails to act in a constructive manner, views foreign policy through domestic political lenses, acts unilaterally or at the instigation of special interest groups, and shirks many of its foreign policy responsibilities. These weaknesses hamper Congress's effectiveness and make it more difficult for the president to implement policy.

The basic test for judging any foreign policy decision should be: Does it advance the American national interest? Defining the national interest is difficult, because it includes goals as diverse as protecting the safety of the American people, promoting open international trade, and advancing human rights. Indeed, we have multiple security, political, economic, and humanitarian interests on every continent. The responsibility of a member of Congress is to look at each foreign policy issue and determine how U.S. policy can best advance the broad range of American interests in that issue.

Yet members of Congress sometimes view a foreign policy challenge from a parochial or limited perspective rather than from the broader perspective of the national interest. Too often, members focus on just one aspect of the national interest while neglecting others. For example, some members look at China only in terms of its human rights performance or its export of military technology, giving short shrift to the many other U.S. interests in China, such as economic growth and stability in Asia. Similarly, some members view Turkey only through the lens of its relations with Greece and Cyprus, failing to consider the broader strategic role Turkey plays as a key bridge between the West and the Middle East.

Frequently, Congress gets involved in foreign policy at the instigation of special interest groups. Although Congress should take the views of these groups into account, it too often places their concerns above the national interest. For instance, it sometimes takes an excessively hard line on Cuba because of the electoral and financial clout of Cuban Americans, or it attacks the United Nations because doing so gains favor among some influential constituencies.

On many occasions, the positions of special interest groups are consistent with the national interest. For example, the support of business for open trade helps to promote American prosperity and economic growth. But members of Congress must determine for themselves what the national interest is on a given issue. Their support for, or opposition to, trade agreements should derive not from the lobbying influence of corporations, labor unions, or any other group, but rather from a careful consideration of the overall impact of trade agreements on the full range of U.S. interests.

Too often, members of Congress use foreign policy to score political points by bringing forward bills with little expectation of making law. For example, Congress regularly authorizes money to move the U.S. Embassy in Israel from Tel Aviv to Jerusalem, which most supporters of Israel favor, knowing that the president will waive the legislation because the move would complicate America's position as a mediator between the Israelis and Palestinians. And nearly every year, with the encouragement of Armenian Americans, Congress seeks to approve a resolution recognizing the genocide of Armenians during World War I—even though administrations oppose the resolutions because of the varied U.S. interests in the Eastern Mediterranean and the American desire to avoid alienating Turkey. Members of Congress also sometimes play politics with America's critical bilateral relationship with China by advancing bills that criticize China's policies in a range of areas, from prison labor to abortion, at sensitive moments in U.S.–Chinese relations when other important issues are at center stage.

Some of these congressional deficiencies are similar to Congress's strengths. For instance, the congressional tendency to view foreign policy through domestic lenses and to pursue initiatives favored by interest groups reflects in part the great diversity and variety of perspectives in Congress. Indeed, Congress is performing its constitutional role as the most representative body in government when it advocates on behalf of constituents who advance a particular foreign policy priority. In the domain of foreign policy, however, Congress must place the national interest above self-interest or parochial concerns. Striking the right balance between the promotion of diverse interests and the advancement of the national interest is fiendishly hard to do, but members of Congress must always give the highest priority to the long-term interests of the nation.

Frequently, Congress does not take foreign policy seriously enough or spend sufficient time on it. Except in times of crises, such as in the wake of the September 2001 terrorist attacks, domestic policy is a much higher priority for Congress, as it is for most Americans. In this, Congress is true to its representative nature. Members of Congress usually focus on domestic policy because they know their constituents want them to.

Congress does not always fulfill its constitutional role to be both a critic and a partner of the president. Instead, Congress sometimes does little more than bash the president's policies. Congress has frequently criticized the 1994 Agreed Framework on North Korea, for instance, without either advancing an alternative strategy or withholding funding. Some members of Congress accused President Clinton of bowing to blackmail and appeasing the North Koreans—erroneous judgments, in my opinion—but then demonstrated the hollowness of their denunciations by declining to block administration policy.

Sometimes, Congress undermines U.S. interests by pushing initiatives that damage American relations with other nations or weaken international institutions. Sanctions placed by Congress on Cuba, Iran, and Libya in recent years have strained U.S. ties with allies in Europe, Latin America, and the Middle East while failing to have the desired impact on the targeted regimes. Congressional votes to withhold dues payments to the United

Nations and reject the Comprehensive Test Ban Treaty have also fueled international resentment of the United States and made it more difficult for America to achieve its foreign policy goals.

Congress often shirks its responsibilities in foreign policy. For instance, it regularly fails to authorize or disapprove the use of military force. Congress has authorized the use of force only three times since 1973—in 1983, when U.S. troops were sent to Lebanon; in 1991, on the eve of the Gulf War; and in 2001, following the terrorist attacks on the World Trade Center and the Pentagon. Many other military engagements, including in Grenada, Panama, Somalia, Haiti, Bosnia, and Kosovo, have passed by without congressional votes to either authorize or reject the use of force. Congress frequently prefers to play Monday morning quarterback, letting the president make the tough military decisions, and then criticizing or praising him depending on the results.

Sometimes, congressional actions during a conflict only serve to complicate things for the president. During the 1999 NATO intervention in Kosovo, for instance, Congress acted in a confusing variety of ways. Congress did not declare war or authorize the bombing campaign, but it also declined to call for the bombing to stop. One day, the House voted that President Clinton could not introduce ground troops into the conflict without congressional approval; the next day, a House committee voted to give the president twice as much money as he had requested for the military operation. These apparently contradictory actions left the American people and foreign leaders wondering where Congress stood. Voting on issues of war and peace is not easy—indeed, the decision to intervene militarily overseas is the most difficult decision our government can make—but Congress has a responsibility to try to forge a consensus and develop a coherent policy.

Congress also has a poor record of considering international treaties that have been signed by U.S. presidents and await Senate ratification. In some cases, when the Senate votes to reject a treaty, it is asserting its independent judgment, which is its proper constitutional role. But dozens of treaties signed by U.S. presidents and submitted to the Senate during the past fifty years have simply been collecting dust and have not even been taken up for debate—on issues ranging from human rights, to the environment, to maritime regulation. When the Senate fails to consider treaties properly, it neglects its constitutional responsibility and encourages the president to rely more on executive agreements that do not need congressional approval.

Another important responsibility of the Senate is the approval of foreign policy appointments. Yet the amount of time taken to confirm appointments has grown steadily, and numerous key appointments have been held up, often by individual senators, for frivolous, partisan, or unrelated reasons. For thirteen months during President Clinton's second term, the United States was without an ambassador to the United Nations because Richard Holbrooke's nomination was held up due to partisanship and congressional hostility to the United Nations. President George W. Bush's nominee for assistant secretary of state for Latin America, Otto Reich, was not given a hearing by the Democratic-led Senate for most of 2001, and Bush resorted to appointing him when Congress was out of session to install him in the post. Serious questions or concerns about a nominee for a government post should be pursued—and there were legitimate concerns about Reich—but most nominees, whose qualifications for the job are not in doubt, should be confirmed by the Senate promptly. If a nomination is tied up in committee, it should go to the Senate floor after a reasonable period of time for an up-or-down vote—because long vacancies in key positions can seriously damage U.S. foreign policy.

Sometimes, Congress acts too timidly in foreign policy by passing the buck. Take its approach to economic sanctions, which it has enacted frequently during the past decade. Congress approved more sanctions legislation during the 1990s than during the previous eighty years. This record may suggest that Congress is acting more forcefully in foreign policy, but in fact it is often posturing and attracting credit for acting tough by enacting sanctions legislation while placing the entire burden of making the difficult decision to impose sanctions on the president. Congress often leaves it to him to determine whether to apply or waive sanctions if U.S. law has been violated. Congress thus punts the issue to the president and forces him to take the political heat that may follow his decision, rather than sharing the responsibility with him.

Congress also neglects its foreign policy responsibilities by failing to spend enough time rigorously overseeing foreign policy. Congress must do more than write the laws; it must make sure that the administration is carrying them out the way it intended. In recent years, it has devoted little time to rigorous programmatic oversight, focusing instead on personal investigations often designed to discredit individual public officials.

Conversely, Congress too often micromanages foreign policy. Administrations often criticize Congress for this—and sometimes rightfully so. Congress frequently fills bills with detailed performance and reporting requirements that can excessively restrict the president's flexibility in implementing policy and consume enormous amounts of time in the executive branch. Secretary of Defense Donald Rumsfeld noted with dismay in 2001 that the Defense Department is required to file some 900 reports with Congress. The production of these reports occupies a large army of people in the Pentagon, yet many of the reports pile up without being read on Capitol Hill. Oversight is an important function of Congress, but it should not place unnecessary burdens on the executive. In Congress's defense, micromanagement often results from executive abuse or congressional frustration with a failure of the executive to consult with Congress and take its concerns into consideration.

Congress sometimes makes it more difficult to formulate foreign policy by linking unrelated issues together, rather than considering them on their individual merits. During the 1990s, for instance, Congress linked funding for the United Nations to abortion. Some members of Congress who favored paying U.S. dues to the United Nations in full and on time were forced to vote against dues payments because they opposed the linked legislation restricting the right of aid organizations to provide assistance for abortions overseas. When Congress links tough foreign policy issues to other controversial measures, it makes it all the more difficult to move forward on them.

It is far more easy—and more common—for Congress to block a foreign policy bill than to enact new legislation. In the Senate, particularly, where filibusters and holds by individual senators can occur, it can be extremely difficult to pass foreign policy measures. Thirty years ago, filibusters were rare, and primarily occurred on issues of major constitutional importance. Today, they, and the threat of them, are a common way to frustrate the majority's will and the greatest source of institutional gridlock in Washington. The number of filibusters per Congress rose from an average of one during the 1950s to twenty-nine in the 105th Congress of 1997–99. If senators do not have enough support to sustain a filibuster, they sometimes resort to placing a hold on foreign policy legislation or appointments. These holds can allow one senator to block the rest of the Senate from acting on important bills or nominations.

Congress also makes it difficult to advance foreign policy objectives by providing insufficient resources for foreign policy. It insists on strong U.S. leadership but is often reluctant to support it financially, except for defense. When the federal budget is tight—as it often is—spending on international affairs is frequently one of the first targets for cuts. Since the mid-1980s, funding for diplomatic representation, foreign aid, international exchanges, public diplomacy, and international institutions has declined or frequently been under attack. It is penny-wise and pound-foolish to think the United States can advance its interests around the globe without sufficient resources to promote them.

Yet, though Congress often shortchanges U.S. diplomacy, it frequently appropriates more money than needed for some defense programs. Sometimes, the president wants to streamline the military by closing superfluous military bases and terminating unnecessary weapons programs, but Congress insists on continuing them to protect jobs in members' districts. In 2001, for instance, the Pentagon announced plans to close a number of the country's 398 domestic bases and to shift funds to other programs to meet new threats. Republican and Democratic members of Congress with bases in their districts immediately criticized the plans and attempted to block them, though Congress eventually agreed to begin a new round of base closings in 2005. Members of Congress generally have a responsibility to protect the interests of their constituents. But when it comes to foreign policy and national security, their first responsibility is to the broader interests of the nation.

Finally, despite its increased activism in recent decades, Congress rarely leads and often falls short in educating the American people about foreign policy. It is generally reactive rather than proactive—dealing with foreign policy issues only when forced to by the president or the media. Two of the few recent instances when it initiated policy were its adoption of sanctions against South Africa in protest of apartheid and its crafting of the Cooperative Threat Reduction Program to safeguard nuclear weapons in the countries of the former Soviet Union. Occasionally, members give foreign policy speeches—some are very good—but they rarely feel any real burden to explain our foreign policy challenges to the American people. The members who do so are a distinct minority.

Improving Congressional Performance

To play a more constructive role, Congress should make several reforms and rethink its approach to foreign policy. It should give more power to the committees that authorize foreign policy; realign committee jurisdiction, so that fewer committees are involved in foreign policy issues; and choose the chairs of key foreign policy and national security committees on the basis of merit rather than seniority. These reforms will be very difficult to achieve because members of Congress and committees naturally resist efforts to decrease their influence. But they are necessary to counter the diffusion of power in Congress, streamline the foreign policy process, and give Congress a greater capacity to develop a consensus.

In addition, Congress should reduce the use of omnibus legislation and the number of Senate filibusters and holds, and it should devote more time to rigorously overseeing foreign policy. Better oversight would improve policy, help to root out fraud and abuse, and restore greater public confidence in Congress by showing that it is taking its responsibilities seriously.

Along with these specific recommendations, there is no substitute for responsible action by individual members of Congress. Members must constantly reach out to the many available resources—such as the Congressional Research Service, the Congressional Budget Office, and experts in think tanks, academia, and the private sector—to educate themselves on the intricacies of foreign policy. They should also travel abroad more and participate in international conferences to gain firsthand insight on other nations and world affairs. Their own initiative, more than any structural or procedural reform, can do the most to improve the performance of Congress.

At its best, the making of foreign policy can be a creative process that transcends self-interest or the goals of special interests and seeks to advance the nation's broader interests. The job of the congressional foreign policy maker is to forge a consensus that advances the national interest out of the American people's many interests and concerns. I have always felt that in addition to the various groups and constituencies pressuring members of Congress, there is a constituency for the whole that will support policies that place the national interest first. Members must constantly ask what is the total U.S. interest in a given area or issue, and act according to their best understanding of that interest. If they lead on foreign policy and help to educate the American people on international issues, they can build greater support for policies that advance the national interest, as well as the interests of their constituents.

Congress should put aside efforts to score political points, step up to its constitutional obligations, and take a full share of responsibility for the formulation of U.S. foreign policy. When it does so, it can bring fresh ideas to the policy debate, refine and improve presidential proposals, make U.S. policy more representative of the various views of the American people, and help to mold diverse perspectives into a consensual policy. The founders delegated important foreign policy powers to Congress so that the people's representatives would play a major role in the protection and advancement of U.S. interests. Our foreign policy works best when the president and Congress work together.

CHAPTER 4

Consultation between the President and Congress

Given their shared responsibilities under the Constitution, improved consultation between the president and Congress is the most effective way to strengthen U.S. foreign policy. This consultation—a process of policy discussion and mutual exchange—can take many forms, including executive branch testimony at congressional hearings, briefings by administration officials, and informal conversations. More important than its form is the attitude of the parties involved. Consultation is most effective when each branch makes a sincere effort to involve the other branch in its decision-making processes.

Good consultation has many benefits. It fosters mutual trust between the president and Congress, keeps the president informed about congressional concerns, helps prevent the two branches from taking policy in different directions, improves the environment for dealing with crises, and discourages Congress from micromanaging programs out of frustration at being excluded.

Consultation with Congress also provides the president with a wider range of perspectives than he may receive from his own advisors. The president is isolated in our system of government. Unlike the British prime minister, he rarely confronts his critics face to face. As Lyndon Johnson's press secretary, George Reedy, once noted, no one tells the president to go soak his head. Cabinet officials and other high-ranking advisors depend on the president's favor, and they usually can decipher the direction in which he wants to go on an issue. Members of Congress, conversely, have an independence from the president that can give their advice added weight. The president may not like, or take, their advice, but his consideration of it is likely to produce better policy.

Consultation does not—and should not—ensure agreement between the president and Congress. Differences often remain, regardless of consultation, especially on the toughest issues. But even on those issues, consultation helps smooth some of the hard edges of disagreement, and it almost always refines and strengthens policy.

Instances of Poor Consultation

The president is the chief architect of U.S. foreign policy, and therefore he has the primary responsibility to initiate consultation. Yet every administration that I have known has consulted inadequately on major foreign policy issues.

The best-known example of poor consultation is Woodrow Wilson's effort to achieve ratification of the

Treaty of Versailles, which included the charter for the League of Nations, following World War I. Wilson failed to involve Congress in the treaty's negotiation and refused to consider several key congressional objections. His high-handed attitude toward Congress was reflected in his book *Constitutional Government*, in which he stated: "One of the greatest of the president's powers . . . is his control, which is very absolute, of the foreign relations of the nation. The initiative in foreign affairs, which the president possesses without any restriction whatever, is virtually the power to control them absolutely." Congress's frustration at being excluded from the process of formulating the framework for postwar peace led many senators to vote against the treaty and thereby block its ratification.

In more recent history, the most prominent examples of poor consultation involve the Vietnam War of the 1960s and 1970s and the Contra War in Nicaragua of the 1980s. The U.S. roles in these conflicts were extremely controversial and had serious political repercussions for the Johnson, Nixon, and Reagan administrations. Consultation on U.S. involvement in Vietnam and Nicaragua stands out because it was not simply poor; it was intentionally poor because the administrations wanted to conceal information from Congress and the public. In both cases, policy was controlled by a small group of high-level officials, and few others either inside or outside the executive branch knew the full extent of the government's activities. Administrations viewed Congress in these instances as a nuisance to be avoided rather than as a partner with its own constitutional responsibilities for the formulation of policy. In congressional hearings that I chaired on the Iran-Contra scandal, Reagan administration National Security Advisor John Poindexter said that he "simply did not want any outside interference" from Congress, and another Reagan official, Oliver North, testified, "I didn't want to tell Congress anything."

The Reagan administration also consulted inadequately on U.S. military activity in El Salvador, Grenada, and Libya. President Reagan did not report to Congress when he increased the number of military advisors in El Salvador, told Congress about the Grenada invasion two hours after he ordered the landing of U.S. troops, and informed Congress of the Libya bombing while U.S. aircraft were on their way.

During the 1990s, the Clinton administration consulted poorly on a number of important issues. Perhaps the most politically damaging one involved the United States–led intervention in Somalia. In October 1993, eighteen U.S. soldiers were killed in Somalia during a botched military operation aimed at apprehending two top lieutenants of a Somali warlord. The tragedy created a media furor, which called for some explanation from the administration. Secretary of Defense Les Aspin and Secretary of State Warren Christopher came to Capitol Hill to brief members of Congress on what had happened, but the briefing failed to explain how the administration planned to proceed in Somalia. Real consultation did not take place, because the administration did not have any proposals to discuss. The briefing inflamed congressional criticism of the administration's policy and eventually cost Aspin his job.

Consultation was also insufficient on U.S. military involvement in Bosnia and Kosovo. Following the end of the war in Bosnia, in late 1995, the Clinton administration decided that the United States would participate in a NATO-led deployment of peacekeepers. The administration did not adequately consult Congress on the decision, and the president did not fully explain the purpose of the engagement. The president also misled Congress by saying the deployment would only be for a year, even though such a short time frame was unrealistic. Then, one year later, while Congress was out of session, the president decided to continue the deployment for another year and a half. Many in Congress believed the decision was intentionally made at a time when Congress could not oppose it. Finally, in early 1998, Clinton told Congress he did not have an ending date for the deployment in mind, and U.S. troops remain in Bosnia to this day. The administration managed to get its way on this issue despite poor consultation, but it paid a high price in lost goodwill among many members of Congress.

During the 1999 crisis in Kosovo, the Clinton administration only consulted sporadically with Congress before the start of the NATO bombing campaign against Serb targets. Once NATO began its air campaign, the administration struggled to gain congressional support, in part because of distrust remaining from the experience with Bosnia. The president exerted strong public and diplomatic leadership in support of the NATO effort, but Congress never authorized the action and the lack of firm congressional backing made it more difficult for the president to claim a strong mandate to carry out the bombing campaign.

On other issues, poor consultation prevented the Clinton administration from achieving its policy goals.

This was the case with its efforts to obtain funding for the United Nations and ratification of the Comprehensive Test Ban Treaty. The administration's effort to build congressional support for full U.N. funding was half-hearted and not sustained, and it did not involve the president sufficiently. On the test ban treaty, the administration was unprepared to deal with strong congressional opposition when the Senate took up the treaty in 1999 because it did not consult enough during the years before the Senate vote. The result was Senate rejection of one of President Clinton's most important foreign policy initiatives.

There are few signs of improvement under President George W. Bush. During his first months in office, members of Congress criticized his administration for consulting inadequately on its plans to transform the military and withdraw U.S. support for the Kyoto Protocol on climate change. Following the September 2001 terrorist attacks, members generally praised the president's leadership, but some complained that the administration did not brief members sufficiently on its intelligence information and its plans to respond to the attacks. Members were particularly angered by Bush's decision in October 2001 to restrict intelligence briefings to just eight congressional leaders. A bipartisan congressional outcry caused the administration to restore access to the briefings to a larger number of members. Bush also failed to involve Congress in his controversial decision to authorize military tribunals to try suspected terrorists.

As the war on terrorism entered a new phase in early 2002 after the U.S. victories in Afghanistan, members of Congress voiced frustration that the Bush administration was asking for huge increases in defense spending without explaining its long-term goals for the war. Senate Majority Leader Tom Daschle said, "Before we make commitments in resources, I think we need to have a clearer understanding of what the direction [of the war] will be." Members from both parties also urged the administration to consult with Congress more frequently on its plans to topple Saddam Hussein.

Executive Shortcomings in Consultation

These examples of poor consultation, and many others, are marked by a number of common executive branch shortcomings in the consultative process. Often, Congress is only informed of executive branch decisions rather than genuinely consulted. Members of Congress are notified of decisions after they have already been made or they are provided with only limited information. I often heard an administration come to Congress and insist there was no alternative to a decision it had made—when, in fact, it was a 55–45 decision within the administration. There are always options in foreign policy.

Administration officials tend to treat Congress as an obstacle to be overcome instead of recognizing that Congress is an independent branch with its own constitutional role in foreign policy. Many officials believe that Congress is ignorant of sophisticated foreign policy issues and only gets in the way of good policy. They are especially reluctant to hear from members in an open-ended discussion. Sometimes, administration officials just go through the motions when meeting with members of Congress, gloss-

ing over issues superficially rather than engaging in a sub-
stantive give-and-take. They prefer highly structured, almost ritualistic, hearings—if they must deal with Congress in some form.

Administrations usually consult only when a crisis is
at hand, and their consultation is rarely sustained. On
many complex foreign policy issues, administrations
must build a strong base of knowledge in Congress over
a period of years so that members are well informed
when the issues come up for a vote or are publicly discussed. But because administrations do not consult Congress often on issues that are not on their immediate
agenda, members are frequently taken by surprise when
an administration suddenly asks them to support something they have heard nothing or hardly anything about.
The failure of successive administrations to educate and
consult members on international financial institutions is
a classic case; no wonder it was so difficult for the Clinton administration to get congressional approval for an
$18 billion International Monetary Fund quota increase
in 1998.

Consultation is often driven by media headlines.
Sometimes, administrations call members to give them a
"heads-up" on an issue because it will be appearing on
television or in the newspapers the next day. These
heads-ups are self-serving; consultation on the eve of a
press leak is not consultation at all.

Administrations frequently weaken consultation by
authorizing only a few officials to discuss a policy. In
several periods of crisis, when administration officials
should have been consulting all over Capitol Hill, I was
distressed to learn that the president trusted only three

or four people to consult. During the months leading up to the Gulf War, for instance, only the secretary of defense, secretary of state, national security advisor, and chairman of the Joint Chiefs of Staff were authorized by President Bush to discuss Iraq policy with members of Congress. This made it difficult for the administration to get its message across to every member.

In addition, administrations too often reach out to only a limited number of members. To be effective, consultation must target different members depending on the issue—for instance, focusing on the ad hoc Caucus on Ireland when dealing with a matter pertaining to Northern Ireland. Administrations do not always recognize which members are concerned with which issues.

Congressional Shortcomings in Consultation

Congress also has several shortcomings when it comes to consultation. Consultation with Congress is difficult because power in Congress is so diffuse and shifts with each issue. In the 1950s and 1960s, the president could consult effectively with Congress simply by talking to a few important congressional leaders and committee chairs, such as Senate Majority Leader Lyndon Johnson, Speaker of the House Sam Rayburn, and the chairs of the House and Senate foreign relations committees. Today, dozens of members of Congress and many congressional committees play important roles in foreign policy. Members are younger, more sophisticated, more active, more diverse, more independent, and less respectful of traditional patterns of authority. There is no single person—or group of people—with whom the president can consult and then conclude that he has gained congressional support.

Congress is often not receptive to consultation. There is a tendency in Congress to want to be briefed by the president, the secretary of defense, or the secretary of state, and an unwillingness to hear from lower-ranking officials. After the 1994 Agreed Framework with North Korea was negotiated, I thought it would be useful for members of Congress to be briefed on the accord because it was of major importance to security in East Asia. I helped organize two briefings for members on Capitol Hill with the State Department official who negotiated the agreement, and only one other member showed up.

Consultation can also be difficult because Congress is frequently poorly informed about foreign policy. Most members focus mainly on domestic issues, and many give little thought to international affairs except when a vote is pending or a crisis breaks. This lack of sustained interest in foreign policy can complicate an administration's effort to consult.

Members of Congress tend to be heavily influenced by special interests, ethnic groups prominent in their districts, and short-term objectives. This narrow perspective can make it difficult for an administration to win support for policies that offer no immediate political benefit to members. Partisanship can further undermine consultation. During the Clinton presidency, the House Republican leadership sometimes refused to be consulted by the administration while Democrats were present, making it far more difficult to develop a bipartisan foreign policy.

Congress's capacity to leak sensitive information to the media can be an additional obstacle to consultation. Fear of leaks can discourage executive branch officials from sharing information with Congress. But administration officials should acknowledge that many leaks come from the executive branch. Administration officials are often skillful at leaking information to Congress and the public to advance their own agendas. I have not seen any evidence that Congress is leakier than the executive.

Instances of Good Consultation

Despite these serious deficiencies in the consultative process, on many occasions consultation has worked well. Most presidents have gained support for their positions on at least some major foreign policy issues by setting their minds to it and working hard to gain congressional backing.

Sometimes, it is relatively easy to consult effectively because Congress and the president are generally in agreement on policy to begin with. Consider NATO expansion. For several years, President Clinton pushed for and achieved the expansion of NATO to include Poland, the Czech Republic, and Hungary. He made a strong case for the expansion, but congressional support for it was solid before his efforts, thanks in part to vigorous lobbying efforts by Polish, Czech, and Hungarian Americans. Public opinion was generally supportive of expansion, and in the 1996 presidential campaign both Clinton and Republican candidate Bob Dole voiced their support for it. The administration therefore had a favorable environment for consultation. In those circumstances, administration officials often like to consult.

A more complicated case is support for U.S. policy toward the Israeli–Palestinian conflict and peace process. To some extent, consultation on the Middle East is relatively easy because most members of Congress are keenly interested in developments there and therefore are eager for consultation. But many members' strong feelings about the Middle East can produce serious differences between members' views and those of the administration. For instance, on many occasions members have pressured an administration to be more supportive of Israel and tougher on its Arab neighbors. Congress has usually supported the president's approach to the Middle East, however, in part because successive administrations have consulted frequently and extensively. When administration officials travel to the Middle East for talks or negotiations, they almost always brief Congress when they return and keep Congress well informed of the latest developments. This consultation is important because it helps sustain congressional backing for the administration's activities and sometimes discourages or deflects unhelpful congressional initiatives.

President Franklin Roosevelt set the standard for effective consultation in modern U.S. foreign policy with his approach to shaping new international institutions following World War II. Roosevelt learned from the mistake Woodrow Wilson had made in consulting Congress insufficiently about the formation of the League of Nations after World War I. Recognizing that he could not achieve his goals for a peaceful postwar international order without the support of Congress, Roosevelt took into account congressional concerns and included prominent members of Congress from both parties in the planning conferences for the United Nations, the International Monetary Fund, and the International Bank for Reconstruction and Development (commonly known as the World Bank). This bipartisan approach helped Roosevelt boost public support for the new international institutions and led the Senate to approve U.S. membership in them by overwhelming margins in 1945. The inclusion of members of Congress in important international conferences and negotiations has been common ever since. Roosevelt's successor, Harry Truman, also consulted effectively to gain congressional approval of important foreign policy initiatives, particularly the treaty establishing NATO and the Marshall Plan providing reconstruction and development aid to Europe.

The most difficult tests of consultation are those in which the president must overcome strong opposition to his proposals. In the late 1970s, President Carter consulted very effectively on two important and controversial issues: turning the Panama Canal over to Panamanian control and selling arms to Saudi Arabia. On both of these sensitive issues, he faced heavy resistance in Congress. At the outset of discussions, most members were generally opposed to giving up control over the canal and were very concerned about arming Saudi Arabia, which they viewed as a potential enemy of Israel.

The administration changed the minds of many members by involving them in the policy-making process and lobbying them aggressively with a variety of techniques. It briefed undecided members of Congress extensively;

distributed detailed notebooks on the issues to members; testified frequently before congressional committees; sent members on visits to Central America and the Middle East; and engaged itself at the highest level, with the president speaking personally with many members. In addition, some senators participated directly in negotiations with Panama over conditions attached to the turnover of the canal. To advance all these consultative efforts, the administration beefed up the congressional relations staff of both the State Department and the White House. Over time, its persistence paid off, as it wore down the opposition and gained congressional passage of its proposals.

More recently, Presidents George H. W. Bush and Bill Clinton consulted effectively to gain congressional support for financial aid to Eastern Europe and the Soviet Union after the fall of communism in those regions. Many members of Congress were initially opposed to giving large amounts of aid to our former enemies, but the administrations presented persuasive arguments for assistance on economic and security grounds and involved Congress heavily in the process of designing the aid programs. This cooperative approach strengthened support in Congress and led to the passage of two major programs to assist the former communist bloc countries.

Bush and Clinton also consulted well to maintain support for preserving normal trade relations with China. This issue was clearly very important to the administrations, which devoted substantial resources to it. The secretary of defense, secretary of state, secretary of the treasury, and U.S. trade representative all traveled regularly to Capitol Hill to explain the benefits of trade with China, and many lower-level officials lobbied heavily as well. My staff and I probably had a dozen meetings a year on the issue with the administrations when I was serving in Congress. During the critical days preceding the annual vote on renewing normal trade relations, Bush and Clinton phoned individual members to lobby for their support.

Guidelines for Good Consultation

These examples of good consultation suggest that the common deficiencies in the consultative process can be overcome, or at least mitigated. The executive and legislative branches can improve foreign policy consultation in ten ways.

First, each branch must understand its proper role, powers, and limitations in foreign policy. The administration must recognize that Congress has an important constitutional role in policy formulation and oversight, and that it can provide policy with stronger public support. Congress must give the executive branch some flexibility in the day-to-day implementation of foreign policy, striking a balance between responsible criticism, based on measured oversight of the executive, and responsible cooperation. There should be an implicit agreement between the branches that if Congress is seriously consulted it will act with some restraint and allow the president to lead. This agreement does not mean that members of Congress should never criticize the president, but rather that they should refrain from obstructing policy without offering constructive alternatives.

Second, the president and Congress must build a relationship based on mutual respect, trust, and partnership. Administration officials must take the perspectives of Congress seriously and respond to congressional concerns. Members of Congress must be sensitive to the complexity of foreign affairs and the difficulty of crafting and implementing policy. The branches must engage in a genuine dialogue on the problems that concern them most.

Third, consultation must take place, to the extent feasible, before decisions, not after they have already been made. Congress should be given a legitimate opportunity to participate in the making of policy. The administration should inform Congress of the range of policy alternatives, and seek Congress's advice. If the administration does intend simply to inform Congress of a decision, it should make this clear and not pretend to be genuinely seeking congressional input.

Fourth, support for consultation must come from the top. Consultation is most effective when the president or other high-level officials are personally involved. The president, his senior national security team, and leaders of Congress must set the example by making consultation a priority and regularly setting aside time for it. Part of the president's leadership must be a clear articulation of what policy is and how the policy is to be implemented, so that administration officials can explain it to members of Congress. For their part, the leaders of Congress must set the example for other members by their constructive approach to the making of foreign policy. They should welcome administration efforts to consult and be willing to help the administration understand the many perspectives of members.

Fifth, consultation must be bipartisan. An administration cannot sustain support for a foreign policy in one party alone; it needs bipartisan backing. Yet, too often, calls for bipartisanship from the executive branch are in reality simply appeals for the opposing party in Congress to approve the administration's agenda. Real bipartisanship means engaging the other party in policy formulation. Congress must also strive for bipartisanship. It is most effective in advancing a foreign policy position when that position has strong support in both parties.

Sixth, the administration must devote more resources to consultation. The 535 members of Congress cannot be reached by just a few administration lobbyists. The administration should increase the number of people working to consult with Congress; assign high-quality people to that task; and frequently send mid-level, as well as high-level, officials to Capitol Hill. It should also keep closer track of the foreign policy views and concerns of every member of Congress. In addition, more former members should be hired to work in the executive branch to improve understanding and strengthen ties between the branches.

Seventh, the administration must have a sustained focus on consultation. It should not focus on consultation only during crises or when it needs immediate congressional support. Congressional support in crisis situations will be more forthcoming if Congress is kept aware of issues before they become crises. On critical and complex issues like China, Russia, and the international financial institutions, the administration should begin to educate members as soon as they enter Congress. The administration must build ties in calm periods so that it has a good rapport with members and access to them when a crisis develops.

Eighth, the administration must consult in many different ways and have a flexible approach. It must recognize the particular form of consultation that is appropriate for a given set of circumstances. The kind of consultation required varies from issue to issue, from situation to situation, and from member to member. Some members are as knowledgeable as administration officials on certain issues; others scarcely know of some issues, let alone know much about them. Administration officials must be aware of these differences of knowledge and perspective among members, and adapt their consultation appropriately. One-to-one discussions between officials and members can be especially effective. President Lyndon Johnson was a master at one-to-one meetings because he knew where each member was coming from and what was important to him or her. Armed with that knowledge, he employed whatever argument was best suited to gain the member's support.

Ninth, members of Congress must make consultation a higher priority. They should encourage consultation by attending briefings and displaying interest in foreign policy. When members do attend briefings, they should ask questions and press the administration on issues. Members should be receptive to consultation from mid-level, as well as high-level, officials, and should hire more former executive branch officials in order to give themselves a deeper understanding of the workings and perspective of an administration.

Tenth, Congress should create a permanent foreign policy consultative group of congressional leaders. In 1993, I joined several other members of the House in introducing a bill to establish such a group made up of the congressional leadership and the chairs and ranking members of the main committees involved in foreign policy. Other members with a special interest or expertise could join the group's work on certain issues. The group would meet regularly—perhaps as often as once a month—with the administration's top foreign policy officials, including the secretary of state, the secretary of defense, and the director of central intelligence. The agenda for these meetings would not be strictly limited, so that members could raise issues they were concerned about. The group would also meet on an emergency basis whenever there was an international crisis or the president was considering military action abroad.

Such a group would enable the executive to consult with a wide range of congressional leaders in a single setting, mitigating its problem of being unable to consult with the diffuse Congress. The group would encourage congressional and administration leaders to work through important policy questions together and would provide a centralized forum for policy discussions and for disseminating appropriate information to other members.

Improved consultation will not end differences and conflicts between the president and Congress over foreign policy. Often, they will differ on the substance of policy no matter how much consultation takes place. In 1997, for instance, President Clinton and House Speaker Newt Gingrich worked hard to gain congressional passage of fast-track authority for negotiating trade agreements, but they were simply unable to attract enough votes for the legislation to pass.

That kind of failure is to be anticipated in our system of government. Congress has a responsibility to challenge administration proposals with which it disagrees. Good consultation should not always be correlated with congressional support. But more often than not, good consultation does help an administration gain greater backing in Congress. It almost always strengthens policy. The power of the presidency is such that the president is usually given the initiative on foreign policy matters. When he keeps Congress involved in the policy-making process and consults sufficiently, his chances for success with Congress increase.

It is not easy to make the U.S. constitutional system for conducting foreign policy work. But if both the president and Congress understand their respective roles, make a greater effort to work together, and put national interests ahead of partisan or personal concerns, the country will be well served because a stronger and more effective foreign policy will emerge.

CHAPTER 5

✍ Conclusion: Shaping a Twenty-First-Century Foreign Policy

Developing a strong and effective foreign policy is hard under any circumstances. But when the president and Congress work at cross-purposes, it is all the more difficult. The Constitution requires that the president and Congress cooperate in order to exercise their shared responsibilities for the conduct of foreign policy. Sustained consultation is the best means to make our foreign policy machinery work.

The world and the nation's political environment have changed dramatically since I joined Congress in 1965. The superpower rivalry and Cold War that then characterized international relations have been replaced by a more complex and rapidly changing world in which the United States is preeminent but joined by webs of interdependence with other nations. The threat of nuclear annihilation is more distant today, but the threats of terrorism and biological, chemical, and information warfare are more and more real. Environmental degradation, infectious diseases, drug trafficking, and other transnational dangers present challenges that we cannot meet by ourselves. Yet at the same time, before us lie new opportunities to use our influence to shape a more peaceful, prosperous, and democratic world.

The foreign policy relationship between Congress and the president has also evolved. Congress is more assertive and intimately involved in foreign policy today, but its actions are often inconsistent, haphazard, and more obstructive than constructive. The increased activism of Congress has helped make U.S. foreign policy more representative of the diverse views of the American people, and the greater scrutiny placed on the president has helped prevent him from amassing too much unchecked power. But the diffusion of foreign policy authority has made it easier for special interests and domestic politics to take priority over national interests, and it has made the task of achieving a consensus on tough issues more difficult than ever before.

These changes underscore the continued importance of the basic principles that have been the source of a strong foreign policy throughout U.S. history. In today's era of globalization, as in the nation's early days, American foreign policy works best when it is shaped by strong presidential leadership, responsible congressional criticism and partnership, and sustained dialogue and consultation. These are the fundamental and timeless building blocks for an effective foreign policy.

The president and Congress may not, and should not, always agree. But if they fulfill their respective constitutional roles, the creative tension between them should produce a foreign policy that serves U.S. national interests and reflects to the greatest extent possible the views of the American people. The many challenges and opportunities ahead of us require nothing less.

 Index

ABOUT THE CENTER

The Center is the living memorial of the United States of
America to the nation's twenty-eighth president, Woodrow
Wilson. Congress established the Woodrow Wilson Center
in 1968 as an international institute for advanced study,
"symbolizing and strengthening the fruitful relationship
between the world of learning and the world of public
affairs." The Center opened in 1970 under its own board
of trustees.

In all its activities the Woodrow Wilson Center is a
nonprofit, nonpartisan organization, supported financially
by annual appropriations from the Congress, and by the
contributions of foundations, corporations, and individuals.
Conclusions or opinions expressed in Center publications
and programs are those of the authors and speakers and do
not necessarily reflect the views of the Center staff, fellows,
trustees, advisory groups, or any individuals or organizations
that provide financial support to the Center.